CASE STUDIES FOR
INCLUSION IN EDUCATION

CASE STUDIES FOR INCLUSION IN EDUCATION

Strategies and Guidelines for Educating Students with Disabilities in the General Education Environment

By

KEITH STOREY, Ph.D., BCBA-D

Juvo Autism and Behavioral Health Services
Oakland, CA

CHARLES C THOMAS • PUBLISHER • LTD.
Springfield • Illinois • U.S.A

Published and Distributed Throughout the World by

CHARLES C THOMAS • PUBLISHER, LTD.
2600 South First Street
Springfield, Illinois 62704

© 2020 by CHARLES C THOMAS • PUBLISHER, LTD.

ISBN 978-0-398-09340-2 (paper)
ISBN 978-0-398-09341-9 (ebook)

Library of Congress Catalog Card Number: 2020018159 (print)
2020018160 (ebook)

With THOMAS BOOKS *careful attention is given to all details of manufacturing
and design. It is the Publisher's desire to present books that are satisfactory as to their
physical qualities and artistic possibilities and appropriate for their particular use.*
THOMAS BOOKS *will be true to those laws of quality that assure a good name
and good will.*

Printed in the United States of America
MM-C-1

Library of Congress Cataloging-in-Publication Data

Names: Storey, Keith, 1956– author.
Title: Case studies for inclusion in education : strategies and guidelines
    for educating students with disabilities in the general education
    environment / by Keith Storey.
Description: Springfield, Illinois : Charles C Thomas, Publisher, Ltd.,
    2020. | Includes bibliographical references and index.
Identifiers: LCCN 2020018159 (print) | LCCN 2020018160 (ebook) |
    ISBN 9780398093402 (paperback) | ISBN 9780398093419 (ebook)
Subjects: LCSH: Children with disabilities—Education—Case studies. |
    Inclusive education—Case studies. | Special education—Case studies.
Classification: LCC LC4015 .S765 2020 (print) | LCC LC4015 (ebook)
    | DDC 371.9—dc23
LC record available at https://lccn.loc.gov/202001859
LC ebook record available at https://lccn.loc.gov/202001860

I have been fortunate to finish my career working at Juvo Autism and Behavioral Health Services. A great place to work and full of very talented, very bright, and very young (!) people. I dedicate this book to the clinical staff that I worked directly with on cases: Clara Ackerman, Shelby Beauchamp, Sasha Benwell, Jenifer Caceras, Melissa Colmenares, Katheryn Craytonshay, Iyana Davis-Johnson, Erika Dawn, JC Escobar, Shanine Evangelists, Paula Fortune, Michelle Garibay, Martha Gonzalez, Alissa Greenberg, Allison Harger, Erwin Higueros, John Hines, Melinda King, Anita Lind-Mikkelsen, Kana Lopez, Jess Magallon, Alexis Marona, Jessica Martinez, Cedric McBane, Maddy McClinton, Autumn McCloskey, Zulema Montes De Oca, Philip Moore, Kristin Ojala (the best supervisor that I had in my career), Jeffrey Paular, Joan Phillips, William Railson, Janide Reyes, Sheri Roberson, Norma Sanchez, Devra Sholinbeck, Dami Shonaike, Jessica Victor, Jamie Wilson, Adriel Wong, and Jai Yee. And a special thanks to Dr. Mel Dauster.

PREFACE

Scope

The intent of this book is to serve as a guide for teachers, teachers in training, and other service providers to engage in understanding and analyzing inclusion to help prepare them for how they can best teach and serve all students, including those with a disability. These case studies provide a guide for analyzing real life situations and will help readers to become a better teacher and service provider. Too often the inclusion planning process only looks at a few areas and not a comprehensive analysis of skill and support needs. This book provides the framework for analyzing these areas.

My approach is to write in a non-technical style and provide case study examples and guides for assisting readers in analyzing and understanding appropriate supports and interventions for inclusion. In this book, I provide a system for teachers, teachers in training, and others (school psychologists, behavior specialists, classroom assistants, etc.) to analyze inclusion and to understand how supports and instruction can be used to best educate students with disabilities.

Purpose

This book responds to a critical need for highly qualified personnel who will become exemplary professionals in inclusive education for students with disabilities because of their advanced knowledge, skills, and experiences in working with students with varying disabilities. The exploration of inclusion needs to be situated within a context, which, in this book, is the use of the case studies for understanding and analysis.

An advantage of this book is that universities, school districts, and organizations preparing teachers can easily use it in courses or trainings that address inclusive education as the case studies comprehensively cover methodology and issues that represent best practices and evidence-based methods in this area. Those who are already teachers or other support providers will find the case studies to be practical and helpful for increasing their skills in applied settings. I see three main groups who would primarily be interested in this book:

The first is teachers (or other professionals) in training (college teacher preparation programs). The second is teacher (or other professionals in the field) who are interested in learning more about inclusion or are involved in teacher in-service training regarding inclusion. The third group is college instructors teaching courses in Inclusive Education. College instructors are likely to choose the book based upon:

a. The consistent format throughout the book.
b. The "practicality" and "readability" of the book for students in college.
c. The comprehensive analysis and coverage of developing supports and services for students with disabilities.
d. The direct applicability of the case studies to applied settings.
e. The ability to use the case studies as assignments and/or exams.

Plan

There are 10 case studies in the book with five providing complete analysis and five that provide a description of the case with the components for analysis that readers can use for their own education and that professors or other instructors can use in courses and/or trainings.

What it covers:
1. Overview of Inclusion
2. Overview of Case Studies
3. Five Case Studies with Complete Analysis
4. Five Case Studies with Partial Analysis
5. Appendix A: General References Related to Inclusion of Students with Disabilities
6. Appendix B: Organizations and Resources Regarding Inclusion
7. Appendix C: Empirical Research to Support that the Interventions Used in the Case Studies are Evidence-Based Practices

CONTENTS

SECTION ONE–
CASE STUDIES WITH COMPLETE ANALYSIS

SECTION TWO–
CASE STUDIES WITH PARTIAL ANALYSIS

CASE STUDIES FOR INCLUSION IN EDUCATION

OVERVIEW OF INCLUSION FOR STUDENTS WITH DISABILITIES

What is a Disability?

Students with a disability may be classified as having one (or more) of thirteen categories according to the Individuals with Disabilities Education Act of 2004 (http://idea.ed.gov) (other legislation and laws may have different disabilities categories and definitions). These are:

Autism
Deaf-Blindness
Deafness
Emotional Disturbance
Hearing Impairment
Intellectual Disability
Multiple Disabilities
Orthopedic Impairment
Other health Impairment
Specific Learning Disability
Speech or Language Impairment
Traumatic Brain Injury
Visual Impairment, Including Blindness

These disabilities can occur in combination within an individual; for example, a student can have a Learning Disability and a Visual Impairment though only one disability is their "primary disability" in order to received special education services. Table 1.1 provides terms and definitions regarding disability and other related terms.

Table 1.1
TERMS AND DEFINITIONS

DISABILITY:	Refers to an attribute of a person. A functional limitation that interferes with a person's ability to walk, hear, talk, learn, etc.
HANDICAP:	Refers to the source of limitations (e.g., attitudinal, legal, and architectural barriers), a situation or barrier imposed by society, the environment, or oneself.
IMPAIRMENT:	Implies diseased, damaged, or defective tissue.
DISORDER:	An upset of health or functioning. To disturb the normal physical or mental health of; to derange.
EXCEPTIONAL:	Any student whose physical attributes and/or learning abilities differ from the norm, above or below, enough so that an individualized program of special education is required.
HIDDEN DISABILITY:	A disability which is not physically/visually apparent.
TEMPORARILY ABLE BODIED:	A person who is currently without a disability.
HANDICAPISM:	A set of assumptions and practices that promote the differential and unequal treatment of people because of apparent or assumed physical, mental, or behavioral differences. (Bogdan & Biklen, 1977).
MEDICAL MODEL:	Disability is considered a defect or deficiency that can be located within the person and primary emphasis in on the etiology or causes of organic conditions that permit persons with different types of disabilities to be placed in separate diagnostic categories. A person's disability is a personal medical problem, requiring a medical solution.
ABLEISM:	A pervasive system of discrimination and exclusion that oppresses people who have mental, emotional and physical disabilities. . . . Deeply rooted beliefs about health, productivity, beauty, and the value of human life, perpetuated by the public and private media, combine to create an environment that is often hostile to those whose physical, mental, cognitive, and sensory abilities . . . fall out of the scope of what is currently defined as socially acceptable." [Rauscher & McClintock (1996). p. 198].

Table 1.1—*Continued*

NEUROTYPICAL SYNDROME:	Neurotypical syndrome is a neurobiological disorder characterized by preoccupation with social concerns, delusions of superiority, and obsession with conformity. Neurotypical individuals often assume that their experience of the world is either the only one, or the only correct one. NTs find it difficult to be alone. NTs are often intolerant of seemingly minor differences in others. When in groups NTs are socially and behaviorally rigid, and frequently insist upon the performance of dysfunctional, destructive, and even impossible rituals as a way of maintaining group identity. NTs find it difficult to communicate directly, and have a much higher incidence of lying as compared to persons on the autistic spectrum. NT is believed to be genetic in origin. Autopsies have shown the brain of the neurotypical is typically smaller than that of an autistic individual and may have overdeveloped areas related to social behavior. Tragically, as many as 9625 out of every 10,000 individuals may be neurotypical. There is no known cure for Neurotypical Syndrome. (http://isnt.autistics.org)

What is Inclusion?

Students with disabilities have always been in general education environments. However, with greater awareness and knowledge of disabilities, an increase in legal rights of students and their parents, the availability of better diagnostic services, and more emphasis on providing for individual differences and abilities within the general education environment (for all students, with or without a disability which is known as "universal design"), students with disabilities have become a more recognizable part of the school population. Disability may be seen as part of the cultural and ethnic mix of students and well as part of the diverse learning styles and abilities of all students (Baglieri & Shapiro, 2012; Valle & Connor, 2010).

Inclusion has been difficult to define and measure. No single definition of inclusion enjoys consensus and a comprehensive definition has been elusive. Ford and Davern (1989) pointed out that inclusion is a complex social phenomenon while Mank and Buckley (1989) described inclusion as "in its simplest and most elegant form as a degree of community presence and participation for persons with disabilities that is no different from that enjoyed by persons without a disability label" (p. 320). Table 1.2 provides different definitions of inclusion that have been provided over the years in the professional literature.

Table 1.2
DEFINITIONS OF INCLUSION

1. "Inclusion . . . means that students attend their home school with their age and grade peers. . . . Included students are not isolated into special classes or wings within the school. To the maximum extent possible, included students receive their in-school educational services in the general education classroom with appropriate in-class support." (National Association of State Boards of Education, 1992, p. 12).

2. "Inclusion is a shared value which promotes a single system of education dedicated to insuring that all students are empowered to become caring, competent, and contributing citizens in an integrated, changing, and diverse society." (Kukic, 1993, p. 3).

3. "An inclusive classroom setting is one in which the members recognize each other's individual differences and strive to support one another's efforts." (Putnam, 1993, p. xiii).

4. Full inclusion is "an approach in which students who are disabled or at risk receive all instruction in a regular classroom setting: support services come to the student." (Hardman, Drew, Egan & Wolf, 1993, p. 485).

5. Partial inclusion involves a student receiving most of their instruction in regular education settings, but the student may be "pulled out" to another instructional setting when it is deemed appropriate to their individual needs." (Hardman, 1994, p. 5).

6. Inclusion is the term most commonly applied to the practice of educating students with moderate to severe disabilities alongside their chronological age peers without disabilities in general education classrooms within their neighborhood schools. Inclusion includes physical integration, social integration, and access to normalized educational, recreational, and social activities that occur in school. Inclusion does not necessarily imply that all students with disabilities will spend all day every day in a general education class or learn exactly the same things at the same mastery level as students without disabilities. (Alper, 2003, p. 15).

7. In the inclusive school, all students are educated in the general education programs. Inclusion is when a student with special learning and/or behavioral needs is educated full time in the general education program. Essentially inclusion [italics in original text] means that the student with special education needs is attending the general school   p r o - gram, enrolled in age-appropriate classes 100% of the school day. (Idol, 2006, p. 4).

8. . . . that students with disabilities are served primarily in the general education classroom under the responsibility of the general classroom teacher. (Mastropieri & Scruggs, 2010, p. 7).

9. . . . all learners are welcomed full members at their schools and in the classrooms and that they are seen as the responsibility of all educators. It further implies that educators' strong preference is for these students to be educated with their peers without disabilities. (Friend & Bursuck, 2012, p. 6).

Thus, inclusion in educational settings involves students with disabilities participating in instruction and activities in the general education classroom and throughout their school communities (e.g., in the lunchroom, in school clubs, etc.). This book is based on the premise educating students with disabilities in the general education environment (with appropriate supports) is a good thing.

Components of Inclusion

Five components of inclusion have been promoted (Mank & Buckley, 1989; Storey, 1993). These are physical inclusion, social inclusion, relationships, social networks, and academic inclusion.

Physical Inclusion

Physical inclusion is a necessary first step for the other components of inclusion to occur. Physical proximity is a basic assumption for inclusion; in other words, the student with a disability has to be physically present in the general education classroom for other types of inclusion to occur. Without physical inclusion there cannot be social integration, relationships, social networks, and academic inclusion. But mere physical presence may not necessarily lead to other forms of inclusion. For example, a student with a disability may attend a general education class but be seated in the back of the room with a one on one classroom assistant and be doing academic work that is different from the other students in the class. This would be a physically inclusive setting but a socially and academically segregated situation.

Social Inclusion

Social inclusion involves elective personal interactions and has been defined as regular access to interactions with individuals without a disability and regular use of normal community resources (Will, 1984). Therefore, for social inclusion to occur, interactions between the student with a disability and non-disabled peers are a necessary condition. Social interactions have been found to predict likability and friendship patterns (Gresham, 1982), are often conceptualized as forms of conversation and communication (Certo & Kohl, 1984), and competent social interactions elevate social perceptions of persons with disabilities (Gaylord-Ross & Peck, 1985).

Relationships

Relationships depend upon ongoing social interactions and usually involve reciprocal participation in activities (Mank & Buckley, 1989). Social relationships are often defined in connection to social support and may be analyzed in terms of quantity, structure, and function (House & Kahn, 1985). It has been theorized that social interaction progresses in stages (Shelden & Storey, 2014; Trower, 1979). Relationships and friendships move from formality to intimacy, at each stage exchanging quite different information, making different inferences, and filtering potential friends before allowing deeper levels of intimacy to develop (Stainback & Stainback, 1987).

Social Networks

Social networks involve repeated contact with a number of people who identify the relationships that exist within the group as "socially important." The interactions are characterized by reciprocity among members and occur in a variety of settings. Social networks generally refer to the people identified as socially important to a person (Barrera, 1986). Mank and Buckley (1989) refer to social networks as involving "repeated contact with a number of people who identify the relationships that exist within the group as 'socially important'" (p. 320). Social contact patterns and social supports are directly related to social networks and are often conceptualized under the term "social life" (Kennedy, Horner, & Newton, 1989). Social networks generally have been assessed by measuring the size, structure, functions, and adequacy of the network (Calder, Hill, & Pellicano, 2012; Simplican, Leader, Kosciulek, & Leahy, 2015). Self-fulfillment and satisfaction with one's quality of life have been highly associated with a stable social network (Borgatti, Everett, & Johnson, 2013; Haring, 1991).

Academic Inclusion

This involves access to normalized educational instruction and activities that occur in school. This includes access to the general education curriculum with most of the student's academic instruction occurring in the general education classroom. Oh-Young and Filler (2015) found that research indicates that the majority of students with disabilities in more integrated settings outperform those in less integrated settings on both academic and social outcome measures.

How do Mainstreaming, Least Restrictive Environment, and Exclusion Differ from Inclusion?

What is Mainstreaming?

Mainstreaming is when students with disabilities spend most of their time in a segregated classroom (one serving only students with disabilities) and then are selectively placed in one or more general education classes. The expectation for mainstreamed students is that they achieve academically and socially at a level that is similar to that of the students without a disability in that class. While some accommodations or modifications may be made, the curriculum goals of the general education class are also the goals for the mainstreamed student.

The assumption with mainstreaming is that the students with a disability must *earn* their opportunity to be in the general education environment through the ability to "keep up" with work assigned by the teacher for the other students in the class. This is in contrast to inclusion where the expectation that the student with a disability will spend most of or all of his or her time in the general education setting with appropriate support. In other words, with mainstreaming the student with a disability is based in the special education classroom and moves into the general education classes for part of their day. With inclusion the student with a disability is based in the general education classroom but may be pulled out for other things such as extra instruction on reading, mobility training, or instruction of functional skills in the community (Storey & Miner, 2017).

Mainstreaming has sometimes been described as "Islands in the Mainstream" where the special education programs are located in the regular education building but are perceived as separate from the mainstream of school life with separate educational and social activities. With mainstreaming the school administrators and teachers often do not provide support for inclusion. They may recognize inclusion, even speak positively of it, but the ability to make inclusion (or even mainstreaming) work generally depends upon the individual teachers who make it work.

What is the Least Restrictive Environment?

According to the text of the legislation (Individuals with Disabilities Education Improvement Act of 2004, http://idea.ed.gov):

[Least restrictive environment means that] to the maximum extent appropriate, children with disabilities, including children in public or private institutions or other care facilities, are educated with children who are not disabled and special classes, separate schooling, or other removal of children with disabilities from the regular education environment occurs only when the nature or severity of the disability is such that even with the use of supplementary aids and services, education cannot be achieved satisfactorily. The placement of an individual student with a disability in the least restrictive environment shall:

1. provide the special education needed by the student
2. provide for education of the student to the maximum extent appropriate to the needs of the student with other students who do not have disabilities
3. be as close as possible to the student's home.

In addition, the regulations refer to LRE in terms of inclusion into at least three school environments:

- The general education class (academic integration)
- Extracurricular activities (school-sponsored clubs and sports)
- Other nonacademic activities (recess, mealtimes, transportation, dances, and the like)

It is the decision of the Individual Education Team, through an Individual Education Plan (IEP), that decides what the LRE is for each student. This decision can vary greatly across (or within) a district as well as from (or across districts) one district to another. For example, District A may decide that the LRE for a specific student is 100% of her time in a general education classroom with appropriate supports. That same student can move to District B that is next to District A and District B can decide that the LRE is a placement in a classroom serving only other students with disabilities. It is the same student but two different interpretations of what is a LRE for that student.

The Least Restrictive Environment indicates that students with disabilities should be included in the general education curriculum and classroom "to the maximum extent appropriate." The LRE legislation and legal cases however also support the continuum of alternative placements for students with disabilities (Turnbull & Turnbull, 1998).

Pitfalls of LRE

As Shyman (2015) points out that the concepts of "greatest extent" and "appropriateness" in and of themselves, lack guidelines, and each one on its own can be the very issue that creates the controversy in the application of Least Restrictive Environment. Taylor (1988) has discussed various pitfalls and concerns with LRE and the continuum of services concept. These are:

1. The LRE principle legitimates restrictive environments.
2. The LRE principle confuses segregation and integration on the one hand with intensity of services on the other.
3. The LRE principle is based on a "readiness model."
4. The LRE principle supports the primacy of professional decision making.
5. The LRE principle sanctions infringement on people's rights.
6. The LRE principle implies that people must move as they develop and change.
7. The LRE principle directs attention to physical settings rather than to the services and supports people need to be integrated into the community.

What is Exclusion?

Exclusion is a dual system of education where students with disabilities receive their education is schools that serve only students with disabilities (Ferri & Connor, 2006). This education often occurs where students with disabilities are housed in separate areas of a school or in a separate school altogether. The opportunities for inclusion in these settings are often very limited.

Basic Principles Underlying Inclusion

With inclusion the value is that all students belong and that all students are welcome. This includes students with disabilities. Inclusion is focused on the education program and teaching fitting the student rather than student fitting the program (as with mainstreaming). We believe that inclusion needs to be the first option considered as the most appropriate placement for every student with a disability, not the last.

With inclusion, support services are focused on a "push in" rather than a "pull out" model. In inclusive settings supports follow the student and require only that the student will benefit from being in the general education class. The student with a disability may or may not be expected to "keep up" academically with the other students. The assumption is that students with disabilities will be full and active participants in the general education classroom (as well as other school environments) and will occupy socially valued roles within the school community. The intended outcome of inclusion is for students with disabilities to become a true part or member of the regular education class and the school community and that they learn the skills that have been identified as priority learning needs and included on their Individual Education Plan (IEP). Achievement for the student is measured relative to the IEP goals as well as to the regular education curriculum.

With inclusion, special education is a service, not a place. Services and instruction are designed on supporting the student in general education classes. Inclusion may be seen as the right of the student, not the choice of the teacher. Part of the paradox in analyzing inclusion is that there are often two paradigms operating at the same time. Table 1.3 provides an analysis of the two paradigms. Notice that the exclusionary paradigm is looking at how to find a context to exclude students while the inclusionary program is focusing on supports for students to help them be successful.

Table 1.3
CONTRAST OF DISABILITY PARADIGMS

Characteristic	Exclusionary Paradigm	Inclusionary Paradigm
Definition of disability	An individual is limited by his or her impairment or condition	An individual with an impairment requires an accommodation to perform functions required to carry out life activities
Strategy to address disability	Fix the individual, correct the deficit	Remove barriers, create access through accommodation and universal design, promote wellness and health

Table 1.3—*Continued*

Characteristic	Exclusionary Paradigm	Inclusionary Paradigm
Method to address disability	Provision of educational, medical, psychological, or vocational rehabilitation services	Provision of supports (e.g., inclusion teacher, assistive technology, personal assistance services)
Source of intervention	Special Education professionals, clinicians, and other rehabilitation service providers	General education teachers, non-disabled peers
Entitlements	Eligibility for services based on category of disability	Eligibility for services seen as a legal and a civil right
Role of individual with a disability	Object of intervention, patient, beneficiary	Consumer or customer, empowered peer, decision maker
Domain of disability	A medical "problem" involving accessibility, accommodations, and equity	Both a socioenvironmental issue and a cultural issue

Adapted from Brown (2001).

Inclusion is often seen as being related to other movements for inclusion into society such as the civil rights movement and the women's rights movement (Pelka, 2012; Shapiro, 1993; Stroman, 2003). Table 1.4 provides some quotations related to these movements and inclusion for you to analyze about their connection to the importance of inclusion for students with disabilities.

Table 1.4
QUOTATIONS FOR CONSIDERATION
REGARDING THE IMPORTANCE OF INCLUSION

Quotation	Reference
"To separate them from others of similar age and qualifications solely because of their race generates a feeling of inferiority as to their status in the community that may affect their hearts and minds in a way unlikely ever to be undone." p. 708 decision	From Brown vs Board of Education (1954)

continued

Table 1.4—*Continued*

Quotation	Reference
"Separate educational facilities are inherently unequal."	From Brown vs Board of Education decision (1954)
"I may do well in a desegregated society but I can never know what my total capacity is until I live in an integrated society. I cannot be free until I have had the opportunity to fulfill my total capacity untrammeled by any artificial hindrance or barrier."	Martin Luther King, Jr. (1963/1986)
The process toward integration has followed a well-worn path traveled by several generations of people classified as disabled, in nearly the same sequence of graduates steps experienced by several generations of black students. The process seems to have been: identify, categorize, separate, equalize, integrate. The process for blacks was called *desegregation,* for people with disabilities it is called integration.	Slightly modified from Sailor & Guess (1983, p. 3)
". . . It is perfectly true that almost all of us are guilty of this mental and moral sin—of dividing humanity into our sort and their sort. The divisions can be of any kind - racial, religious, national, sexual, social, intellectual, political. . . . Only a minority—a small minority—in every age has refused to make these divisions. Only a few take people where and how they find them, judging them not by some particular or parochial standard, but by a broader human measurement that encompasses the whole species of mankind."	Harris (1986)
"In Special Education, we have followed the traditional medical model. We have diagnosed and prescribed interventions for each child, as mandated by law, often for services out of the classroom. Problems with the instructional setting have not been analyzed; changes needed in classroom instruction have not been specified; and special education intervention has rarely been targeted to improve learning in the classroom. Children's learning has been jeopardized because the basic system that is ineffective for them is left untouched. Because the child, not the system, is defined as the problem, children remain dependent on special education. . . ." p. 33	Case (1992)
"The fact remains, however, that many of those placed in segregated settings do not have the freedom to refuse." p. 293.	Heshusius (2004)
". . . disability is an evolving concept and that disability results from the interaction between persons with impairments and attitudinal and environmental barriers that hinders their full and effective participation in society on an equal basis with others."	United States Convention on the Rights of Persons with Disabilities preamble "e." (2006)

Benefits of Inclusion

There are many benefits to different groups of people with inclusive education. Perhaps the most positive aspect of inclusion is that it can potentially benefit everyone! Inclusion can result in positive changes in education which opens more options for all students, including those with a disability. We have often ignored these larger issues, believing that if we become better teachers and that if our students learn new skills then we will have done our job. However, it is these larger issues that influence the lives of our students with disabilities, probably more than our teaching ability, and it is within the context of these larger issues that we try to influence a society that is often resistant to the changes we wish to make. As Allport (1954) has noted, no child is born prejudiced and that it is within the context of learning and social structure that prejudice occurs.

As noted by Johnson (2003), non-inclusive education will likely meet the same fate of all segregated programs because it was not seen as for "us" but for "them," it will be resented and any money put into it was seen as taking from us (p. 110). If we are to make "them" the "us," then certainly inclusive education needs to be specifically (intentionally?) promoted in schools.

The following listing of benefits has been adapted from Mihail (2015) and Vandercook (2003).

Benefits for Students with Disabilities

Improved Academic Development

Students with disabilities can benefit academically from being included in the general education environment. Research has found that academic outcomes for students with disabilities have been poor or even "abysmal" (Fuchs, Fuchs, McMaster, & Lemons, 2018, p. 127). Gilmour, Fuchs, and Wehby (2018) in their examination of studies between 1997 and 2016 found that students with disabilities on average were 3.3 years below typically developing peers in reading comprehension. Access to the general education academic curriculum (being taught the same content as that of their non-disabled peers) is very important so that the students with disabilities will be more likely to obtain the academic skills that they need to be successful in future academic environments as well as in society as adults.

Friendships, Relationships, and Social Networks with Peers Without Disabilities

A major goal of inclusion is to encourage friendships and social relationships between students with and without disabilities. Having friends and positive social networks is beneficial for all individuals. Having appropriate role models is more likely to occur in inclusive environments. In inclusive settings there is more likely to be an Increased understanding of peers with special needs. The integration of students with disabilities into the regular education setting positively influences the attitudes of non-disabled students about their disabled peers.

Greater Success as Adults and Preparation for the "Real World"

Inclusion can help prepare students with disabilities for community life as an adult. Learning skills to be successful as an adult starts in many ways at school. Getting along with peers and authority figures, following directions, completing tasks, having knowledge of academic information, and developing marketable job skills are often learned at school.

Access to Academics and Extracurricular Activities Through Universal Design for Learning

In inclusive settings there are often varied learning opportunities where students with disabilities are exposed to a wider range of learning opportunities. Individualized education where programs allow students with disabilities to experience the benefits of participating with peers in general education activities, while attending to their specific learning needs. Extracurricular activities such as clubs or sports teams also offer opportunities for students with disabilities to learn skills and be part of their society.

Better Social Acceptance and Reduction in Negative Stereotypes About People with Disabilities

The development of all students is enhanced by the extent to which they feel a sense of belonging, caring and community in school. Students with disabilities are more likely to be accepted as "us" rather than "them" if they are in inclusive educational settings.

Increased Motivation

Students with disabilities are more likely to be motivated to do well both academically and socially if they have non-disabled peers who are role models for them.

Contribution to Diversity

Diversity is not only based upon ethnicity, racial background, gender, sexual orientation, or national origin. Disability is also part of the mix. Inclusive schools provide the opportunity for students with and without disabilities to experience diversity as a natural part of life in communities.

Appropriate Role Models

As with all groups, students with disabilities need positive role models. While students with disabilities can of course benefit from role models of other people with disabilities (whether they be local people or famous people from history), students without disabilities can often be positive role models and they also serve to provide a reference for "normative" behavior of same-age peers. For example, if a student with Autism Spectrum Disorders is placed in a class where there are only other students with Autism Spectrum Disorders, who will serve as appropriate role models for positive social interactions?

Benefits for Students without Disabilities

Learning That Diversity Exists and Can Be Positive

As students with and without disabilities interact as classmates, friendships can develop. This can lead to a better understanding of diversity among peers and that students with disabilities are people first and more similar than dissimilar.

Academic Benefits for Students Without Disabilities

Push in services (such as reading specialists, speech therapists, and/or behavior specialists) can provide supports for all students, not just those with a disability label. There can be improved academic performance for all students resulting from universal design for learning and differentiated instruction: These strategies meet diverse student needs and allows educational teams to expand the ways in which they effectively teach all students.

Understanding and Appreciating Individual Differences

Inclusive education provides opportunities for students without disabilities to have leadership roles such as peer tutors, cooperative learners, and positive role models.

Increased Empathy, Compassion, and Understanding of Differences in Others

Along with understanding and appreciating differences there is likely to be increased empathy, compassion, and understanding of differences towards students with disabilities by non-disabled peers. It is exclusion that can foster and reinforce negative stereotypes and leads to negative attitudes towards people with disabilities.

Benefits for Teachers

Inclusive school environments promote the use of differentiated instructional strategies that increases the ability to teach diverse student learning needs. Teacher use of accommodations, adaptations, modifications, and differentiated instruction benefit all learners.

This allows educational teams to expand the ways in which they effectively teach all students. There is also more likely to be team building for school improvement: The collaborative teamwork required for inclusive education builds staff relationships that support collegiality and other school-wide initiatives. There is also likely to an increase in the effective use of instructional resources, especially instructional personnel, can be leveraged to create more effective and efficient learning for all students in inclusive schools. In addition, teachers who work together solve more problems than when they work alone.

Increased Collaboration Among All Stakeholders

Teaching can often be isolating where a teacher is expected to be in their classroom by themselves with their students. There can be a sharing and learning of teaching materials and techniques. Inclusion is likely lead to improved collaboration skills.

Co-teaching

Co-teaching involves having a general education teacher and a special education teacher working together in a classroom. There are different models for co-teaching such as Shadow Teaching, One Teach/One Assist, Station Teaching, Complementary Teaching, Parallel Teaching, Supplementary Teaching Activities, Team Teaching, Alternative Teaching (Gable, Korinek, & McLaughlin, 1997). Advantages for co-teaching involve Cooperative Planning, Cooperative Presenting, Cooperative Processing, and Cooperative Problem Solving.

Benefits for Society

There will be increased parental involvement where all parents are more involved with their local schools and communities when their children are included. Support of civil rights for all as inclusion is in part a civil rights issue as well as an educational issue. Students with disabilities are more likely to become contributing members of their society as adults.

References

Allport, G. W. (1954). *The nature of prejudice.* Cambridge, MA: Addison-Wesley.

Alper, S. (2003). The relationship between inclusion and other trends in education. In D. L. Ryndak & S. Alper (Eds.), *Curriculum instruction for students with significant disabilities in inclusive settings* (pp. 13–30). Boston, MA: Allyn & Bacon.

Baglieri, S., & Shapiro, A. (2012). *Disability studies and the inclusive classroom: Critical practices for creating least restrictive attitudes.* New York: Routledge.

Barrera, M. (1986). Distinctions between social support concepts, measures, and models. *American Journal of Community Psychology, 14,* 413–445.

Bogdan, R., & Biklen, D. (1977). Handicapism. *Social Policy, 7,* 14-19,

Borgatti, S. P., Everett, M. G., & Johnson, J. C. (2013). *Analyzing social networks.* Thousand Oaks, CA: Sage Publications.

Brown v. Board of Education, 347 U.S. 483 (1954) (USSC+).

Brown, S. C. (2001). Methodological paradigms that shape disability research. In G. L. Albrecht, K. D. Seelman, & M. Bury (Eds.), *Handbook of disability studies* (pp. 145–170). Thousand Oaks, CA: Sage.

Calder, L., Hill, V., & Pellicano, E. (2012). 'Sometimes I want to play by myself':
Understanding what friendship means to children with autism in mainstream
primary schools. *Autism: The International Journal of Research & Practice, 17,* 296–
316.

Case, A. D. (1992). The special education rescue: A case for systems thinking.
Educational Leadership, 50, 32–34.

Certo, N., & Kohl, F. L. (1984). A strategy for developing interpersonal interaction
instructional content for severely handicapped students. In N. Certo, N. Haring,
& R. York (Eds.), *Public school integration of severely handicapped students: Rational
issues and progressive alternatives* (pp. 221–244). Baltimore, MD: Paul H. Brookes.

Ford, A., & Davern, L. (1989). Moving forward with school integration: Strategies
for involving students with severe handicaps in the life of the school. In R.
Gaylord-Ross (Ed.), *Integration strategies for students with handicaps* (pp. 11–31).
Baltimore, MD: Paul H. Brookes.

Ferri, B. A., & Connor, D. J. (2006). *Reading resistance: Discourses of exclusion in deseg-
regation and inclusion debates.* New York: Peter Lang.

Friend, M.,.& Bursuck, W. (2012). *Including students with special needs: A practical guide
for classroom teachers* (6th ed.). Upper Saddle River, NJ: Pearson.

Fuchs, D., Fuchs, L., McMaster, K., & Lemons, C. (2018). Students with disabilities'
abysmal school performance: An introduction to the special issue. *Learning
Disabilities Research and Practice, 33*(3), 127–130.

Gilmour, A. F., Fuchs, D., & Wehby, J. H. (2018). Are students with disabilities
accessing the curriculum? A meta-analysis of the reading achievement gap
between students with and without disabilities. *Exceptional Children, 85,* 329–246.

Gable, R. A., Korinek, L., & McLaughlin, V. (1997). Collaboration in the schools:
Ensuring success. In J. Choate (Ed.), *Successful inclusive teaching* (2nd ed., pp.
450–471). Boston: Allyn & Bacon.

Gaylord-Ross, R., & Peck, C. A. (1985). Integration efforts with severely mentally
retarded populations. In D. Bricker & J. Filler (Eds.), *Severe mental retardation:
From theory to practice* (pp. 185–207). Reston, VA: Council for Exceptional
Children.

Gresham, F. M. (1982). Social interactions as predictors of children's likability and
friendship patterns: A multiple regression analysis. *Journal of Behavioral Assessment, 4,* 39–54.

Hardman, M. L. (1994). *Inclusion: Issues of educating students with disabilities in regular
education settings.* Boston: Allyn and Bacon, Inc.

Hardman, M. L., Drew, C. J., Egan, M. W., & Wolf, B. (1993). *Human exceptionality*
(4th ed.). Boston: Allyn and Bacon, Inc.

Haring, T. G. (1991). Social relationships. In L. H. Meyer, C. A. Peck, & L. Brown
(Eds.), *Critical issues in the lives of people with severe disabilities* (pp. 195–217).
Baltimore, MD: Paul Brookes.

Harris, S. J. (1986). Dividing the world in half. In S. J. Harris, *Clearing the ground.*
Boston, MA: Houghton Mifflin.

Heshusius, L. (2004). Special education knowledges: The inevitable struggle with the
"self." In D. J. Gallagher, L. Heshusius, R. P. Lano, & T. M. Skrtic (Eds.),

Challenging orthodoxy in special education: Dissenting voices (pp. 283-309). Denver, CO: Love Publishing Company.

House, J. S., & Kahn, R. L. (1985). Measures and concepts of social support. In S. Cohen & S. L. Syme (Eds.), *Social support and health* (pp. 83–108). Orlando, FL: Academic Press.

Idol, L. (2006). Toward inclusion of special education students in general education: A program evaluation of eight schools. *Remedial and Special Education, 27,* 77–94.

Johnson, M. (2003). *Make them go away: Clint Eastwood, Christopher Reeve & the case against disability rights.* Louisville, KY: Advocado Press.

Kennedy, C. H., Horner, R. H., & Newton, J. S. (1989). Social contacts of adults with severe disabilities living in the community: A descriptive analysis of relationship patterns. *Journal of The Association for Persons with Severe Handicaps, 14,* 190–196.

King, M. L. (1963/1986). *The essential writings and speeches of Marin Luther King, Jr.* San Francisco, CA: Harpers.

Kukic, S. (1993). From rhetoric to action: Inclusion in the state of Utah. *Special Educator, 14,* 2–4.

Mank, D. M., & Buckley, J. (1989). Strategies for integrating employment environments. In W. Kiernan & R. Schalock (Eds.), *Economics, industry, and disability: A look ahead* (pp. 319–335). Baltimore, MD: Paul H. Brookes.

Mastropieri, M. A., & Scruggs, T. E. (2010). *The inclusive classroom: Strategies for effective differentiated instruction* (4th ed.). Upper Saddle River, NJ: Merrill.

Mihail, T. (2015). *Myths and facts about supported inclusive education.* Retrieved from http://www.tommihail.net/inclusion_myths.html.

National Association of State Boards of Education. (1992, October). *Winners all: A call for inclusive schools.* Alexandria, VA: Author.

Oh-Young, C., & Filler, J. (2015). A meta-analysis of the effects of placement on academic and social skill outcome measures of students with disabilities. *Research in Developmental Disabilities, 47,* 80–92.

Pelka, F. (2012). *What we have done: An oral history of the disability rights movement.* Amherst, MA: University of Massachusetts Press.

Putnam, J. W. (1993). Foreword. In J. W. Putnam (Ed.), *Cooperative learning and strategies for inclusion* (p. xiii). Baltimore: Paul Brookes.

Rauscher, L., & McClintock, J. (1996). Ableism curriculum design. In M. Adams, L. A. Bell, & P. Griffen (Eds.), *Teaching for diversity and social justice* (pp. 198–231). New York: Routledge.

Sailor, W., & Guess, D. (1983). *Severely handicapped students: An instructional design.* Boston, MA: Houghton Mifflin.

Shapiro, J. P. (1993). *No pity: People with disabilities forging a new civil rights movement.* New York: Times Books.

Shelden, D. L., & Storey, K. (2014). Social life. In K. Storey & D. Hunter (Eds.), *The road ahead: Transition to adult life for persons with disabilities* (3rd ed., pp. 233–254). Washington, DC: IOS Press.

Shyman, E. (2015). Toward a globally sensitive definition of inclusive education based in social justice. *International Journal of Disability, Development and Education, 62,* 351–362.

Simplican, S. C., Leader, G., Kosciulek, J., & Leahy, M. (2015). Defining social inclusion of people with intellectual and developmental disabilities: An ecological model of social networks and community participation. *Research in Developmental Disabilities, 38,* 18–29.

Stainback, W., & Stainback, S. (1987). Facilitating friendships. *Education and Training in Mental Retardation, 22,* 18–25.

Storey, K. (1993). A proposal for assessing integration. *Education and Training in Mental Retardation, 28*(4), 279–287.

Storey, K., & Miner, C. (2017). *Systematic instruction of functional skills for students and adults with disabilities* (2nd ed.). Springfield, IL: Charles C Thomas Publisher, Inc.

Stroman, D. F. (2003). *The disability rights movement: From deinstitutionalization to self-determination.* Lanham, MD: University Press of America.

Taylor, S. J. (1988). Caught in the continuum: A critical analysis of the principle of the least restrictive environment. *Journal of the Association for Persons with Severe Handicaps, 13,* 41–53.

Trower, P. (1979). Fundamentals of interpersonal behavior: A social-psychological perspective. In A. S. Bellack & M. Hersen (Eds.), *Research and practice in social skills training* (pp. 3–40). New York: Plenum Press.

Turnbull, H. R., & Turnbull, A. P. (1998). *Free appropriate public education: The law and children with disabilities* (5th ed.). Denver, CO: Love Publishing.

Valle, J. W., & Connor, D. J. (2010). *Rethinking disability: A disability studies approach to inclusive practices.* New York: McGraw-Hill.

Vandercook, T. (2003). Perspectives on the vision of inclusion: The voices of experience. In V. Gaylord, T. Vandercook, & York-Barr, J. (Eds.), *Impact: Feature Issue on Revisiting Inclusive K-12 Education, 16*(1), 2–3, 30. Minneapolis: University of Minnesota, Institute on Community Integration.

Will, M. (1984). *Supported employment for adults with severe disabilities: An OSERS program initiative.* Washington, DC: Office of Special Education and Rehabilitative Services.

OVERVIEW OF CASE STUDIES

This book is designed to provide detailed case studies that can be used by individuals in the field, students practicing for certification, and university programs that prepare teachers and other education professionals. The examples cover areas that represent best practices and evidence-based practices in the field. There is not necessarily a sequential order in which supports and instruction need to be implemented, and thus the case study areas need to be considered as a potentially comprehensive package. The areas covered are detailed within the sections and cover a broad range of topics necessary for implementation for support of the students with disabilities. Too often the planning process only looks at a few areas and not a comprehensive analysis of skill and support needs. Not all areas necessarily apply to each case study.

Evidence-Based Practices

Evidence-Based Practices refers to instructional practices or interventions that have a large and high-quality empirical basis indicating that they are effective for students with disabilities. Sometimes terns such as best practices, scientifically based strategies, scientifically proven practices, teaching practices that have been proven to work, and empirically supported interventions, are also used. The National Autism Center's National Standards Report (2009) provides a summary of treatments for individuals with Autism Spectrum Disorders. They reviewed the latest research in Autism Spectrum Disorders treatment and through a lengthy and scientific procedure they categorized treatments as "established, emerging, unestablished or ineffective/harmful." Torres, Farley, and Cook (2012) note that using evidence-based practices can help eliminate the guesswork and frustrations in instruction and supports. Using evidence-based practices also obviously in-

creases the effectiveness of the instruction and will result in more efficient use of instructional time and increased quality of life outcomes
for individuals.

This can be seen as understanding the empirical basis for what
works in inclusive education. Bernard Shaw said, "He who can, does:
he who cannot, teaches." But, as Sydney J. Harris (1975) put it, "Let's
revise Shaw's foolish saying to 'He who can, does; he who understands, teaches.'" The intervention procedure that are described in this
book are considered "Established" treatments in the National Autism
Center's National Standards Report (2009) and Appendix A provides
citations from professional journals regarding empirical research doc-
umenting that the interventions used in the case studies are evidence-
based practices. In Appendix A I have deliberately included older
"classic" articles and books that readers may find educative.

Terminology and Wording in Text

I have used "active" wording (what happened or is happening) in
each of the case studies. I use "Person-First" language throughout the
book. The language and words used to describe people has tremen-
dous power. When language is used positively (student with a learning
disability, person diagnosed with ASD, person who is liberated by
using a wheelchair) it can enhance the value that people are given.
When language is used negatively (cripple, retard, handicapped, autistic, low functioning) it can result in the devaluing of people and the
lowering of expectations of what is possible for that person to achieve.
What is written and said can promote positive attitudes about the ability of people or it can marginalize and demean them (Mackelprang &
Salsgiver, 2009; Russell, 1994; Shapiro, Margolis, & Anderson, 1990).
It is important to use terms that are clear, accurate, and unbiased.

References

Harris, S. J. (1975). *The best of Sydney J. Harris.* Boston, MA: Houghton Mifflin.
Mackelprang, R. W., & Salsgiver, R. (2009). *Disability: A diversity model approach in
    human service practice* (2nd ed.). Chicago, IL: Lyceum Books.
National Autism Center (2009). *National standards report.* National Autism Center,
    Randolph: MA.
Russell, M. (1994). Malcom teaches us, too. In B. Shaw (Ed.), *The Ragged Edge: The
    disability experience from the pages of the first fifteen years of the Disability Rag* (pp.
    11–14). Louisville, KY: The Advocado Press.

Shapiro, A., Marglois, H., & Anderson, P. M. (1990). The vocabulary of disability: Critical reading and handicapism. *The High School Journal, 73,* 86–91.

Torres, C., Farley, C. A., & Cook, B. G. (2012). A special educator's guide to successfully implementing evidence-based practices. *Teaching Exceptional Children, 45*(1), 64–73.

Areas for Analysis in Case Studies

Accommodations
Modifications
Instructional Strategies
Supports for Teacher
Support for Peers
Support for Family
Positive Behavior Supports
Social Supports
Social Skills Instruction
Self-Management Strategies
Self-Advocacy
Self-Determination
Person-Centered Planning
Inclusion outside of the Classroom in the School
Inclusion Outside of the School Setting
Executive Functioning
Use of Technology
Physical, Medical, Psychological, or Mental Health Issues
Collaboration
Legal Issues
Discussion Questions

The book includes 10 case studies of individuals with disabilities across age groups. I have collapsed the thirteen disability categories from the Individuals with Disabilities Education Act into ten categories for the case studies. Below is a chart that shows the cases across disabilities and age group that are covered in this book.

Matrix of Case Studies by Age and Disability Provided in the Book

IDEA Category	Complete Case Studies	Partial Case Studies
Autism	Elementary (Emin)	
Deaf-Blindness		High School (Curt)
Deafness and Hearing Impairment		Elementary (Lorelie)

Matrix of Case Studies by Age and Disability Provided in the Book—*Continued*

IDEA Category	Complete Case Studies	Partial Case Studies
Emotional Disturbance	Elementary (Ogodei)	
Intellectual Disability	High School (Rhia)	
Multiple Disabilities	Middle School (Della)	
Orthopedic Impairment and Other Health Impairment		High School (Norma)
Specific Learning Disability	High School (Grigory)	
Traumatic Brain Injury		Elementary (Hubert)
Visual Impairment		Middle School (Yumi)

Section One

CASE STUDIES WITH COMPLETE ANALYSIS

CASE STUDY ONE: Emin

Case Study Covers:

- *Autism Spectrum Disorders*
- *Elementary School*

Emin is in kindergarten and is very bright for his age. He is often described as "precocious." Emin can easily do all of the academic work at the kindergarten level and he does test at the second grade level in most of the subject areas. Emin enjoys interacting with adults at the school though these interactions tend to be monologues delivered by Emin on subjects of interest to him. The adults at school generally find these monologues to be amusing though they do find his talking about light bulbs rather odd. Emin does know a lot about different kinds of light bulbs and he enjoys going to hardware and lighting stores and looking at the different bulbs and finding out information from the workers there.

Though it has been suggested that Emin skip several grades because of his academic skills his parents are against it because of his poor social interaction skills with his same-age peers as well as with adults who do not tolerate his "quirky" behaviors. At school Emin's does not play with age appropriate toys that his peers are playing with and his peers avoid playing with him as he does not play games that they are interested in playing. Emin doesn't mind this and when he is not interacting with adults he plays by himself or reads books in the corner. At home Emin does not play with peers either and does not enjoy going to parks or playgrounds. He is physically uncoordinated and does not enjoy physical activities or sports.

At school, Emin does not handle sudden changes to routines well (fire drills, earthquake drills, shooter drills, etc.). He will become upset and yell derogatory names at adults, lie on the floor, and refuse to par-

ticipate in the activity (he sometimes has to be carried by adults out
of the school). Even minor, pre-planned changes to the schedule (such
as an assembly or a holiday sing along) can throw him off and get him
upset. The staff at school and his parents are concerned about these
behaviors (he reacts the same way at home to changes in routines).
Emin does not have an IEP though he does have a 504 Plan. His 504
plan includes accommodations (changes to the environment and
changes to instruction) with the goal being to remove barriers and give
Emin access to learning. Through his 504 plan, Emin receives support
services from an inclusion specialist, Ms. Pauling, and a behavior specialist, Mr. Barrios. Ms. Pauling focuses on social interaction skills for
Emin and Mr. Barrios on positive behavior supports regarding handling changes to routines.

Accommodations

No academic accommodations are needed for Emin.

Modifications

Due to his positive academic performance Emin does not need any
curriculum modifications at this point in time.

Instructional Strategies

Emin is bright and picks up on academic skills quickly and commonly used instructional strategies are appropriate for Emin. However, he does need specific instruction in other areas such as social
skills and those strategies are outlined below.

Supports for Teachers

Emin's kindergarten teacher, Ms. Haymes, has never had a student
like him in her five years of teaching. Though she appreciates his academic ability and his interest in learning she is unsure about how to
handle his social issues and his rigidity. Though she knows some things
about ASD and has had students with autism in the past, none of them
fit the profile of Emin.

She voices her concerns to Ms. Pauling who is more than happy
to give information on these topics to Ms. Haymes (being sure that
Ms. Haymes is comfortable telling her when she has enough infor-

mation so that she is not overwhelmed with things to read and watch). One book that Ms. Haymes especially appreciates is *The Complete Guide to Asperger's Syndrome* by Tony Attwood which clearly lays out information and advice on what to do in non-technical language.

Support for Peers

Emin's peers are rather leery of him and avoid him if at all possible. In addition to the interventions discussed elsewhere in this case study, Ms. Haymes also takes an indirect route by reading the class a variety of books about differences among children (such as racial, cultural, ethnic, disability, etc.) and she also brings in older children and adults who discuss their differences with the children. Ms. Haymes is sure to bring in a child and an adult with ASD as well. This helps all of the students in the class to get a better understanding of differences between them in a positive way.

Support for Family

Though Emin's family understands what Autism is they are not connected to the larger Autism community. Ms. Pauling helps to connect them with the local autism society chapter where Emin's family can interact and receive support from other parents who have a child on the spectrum and also obtain further information regarding autism.

Positive Behavior Supports

Functions of Behavior: Mr. Barrios conducts observations of Emin using the Functional Analysis Observation Form (O'Neill, Albin, Storey, Horner, & Sprague, 2015). From the data collected it is clear that Emin's behavior in response to changes in routines is escape from the change and that his lack of interactions with peers is also serves an avoidance function.

Skill Building: Positive behavior supports often occur on an antecedent basis and involve skill building. For Emin, Ms. Pauling teaches him the use of a schedule as a guide to initiating activities with peers. This provides information to Emin about what expectations are for what he will be doing.

Emin also needs skills for coping with unexpected changes to routine. Mr. Barrios implements combined strategies of antecedent interventions (practicing beforehand with role playing with prerecorded alarms, and videomodeling of appropriately responding), delivery of reinforcement during the practice, and then extra reinforcement at the end of the practice. This intervention is practice twice a week to fidelity (so that Emin responds correctly and promptly during three consecutive sessions. Then maintenance opportunities are provided once a month so that Emin does not lose the skills due to lack of practice.

Reinforcement: As a reinforce for following the schedule and handling changes in routines, Emin earns special adult time. He is given choices such as helping in the office, reading with the librarian, and helping the janitor with light fixtures.

Social Supports

Ms. Pauling and Ms. Haymes were discussing Emin with the third grade teacher, Mr. Sari, and Mr. Sari recommended that they start a school club on electricity since he has several students in his class who are interested in the topic and that it would mesh nicely with Emin's interest in light bulbs and also help Emin connect with some older students who are more at his academic and intellectual level. Both Ms. Pauling and Ms. Haymes think that this is an inspired idea and the three of them start the club and it is a hit with Emin and the other students as they bring in experts about different aspects of electricity and take some field trips to different sites (and they are sure to include a lighting store as one of the sites).

Social Skills Instruction

The school staff understand that the key social skill that Emin needs is how to positively initiate peers for joining games and social activities. Ms. Haymes understand that not only does Emin need skills but that other students have difficulty in these situations as well and that it would be a good idea to review with the whole class how to include their classmates in a game in class and on the playground. Ms. Haymes decided to work with all the students on how to invite someone to join a game, or ask to join in a game, Ms. Haymes started by reading a story book that was about a child not being included in recess games at school. In the story, the young school children learned how to invite someone to join a game, and they also learned how to appropriately ask to join a game. The class discussed the problem in the story and discussed how they could use the "asking" in both situations. To make sure they really learned "how" to ask from the story, Ms. Haymes conducted a role-play where first she modeled the asking, and then she called on students to model it. Emin also had a turn and asked perfectly in both role-plays. Ms. Haymes also used video modeling strategies for teaching the skills by having students role-play appropriate and inappropriate ways of joining games and activities. The students found this to be very fun and it also provided to review the videos at other times to help with generalization and maintenance. Ms. Haymes also met with Emin at the beginning of each recess for a week, and together they watched the videos. During the video watching, Ms. Haymes pointed out to Emin (who was highly focused on the video) the steps he was seeing modeled. With the help of the video and some reminders from his classmates, Emin's positive social behavior did increase (Ms. Haymes made sure to check in with all of the students about their initiating behavior at recess and to praise and reinforce all of the students with good behavior coupons for asking appropriately to join in games), and in a couple of weeks Emin could be seen joining in games at the beginning of recess, just like his peers. Ms. Haymes was able to video Emin using his new learned social skill. These videos became part of the class library video role model collection. The collection was posted on a private class website so students could look at them at any time. The video turned out to be popular as the students loved to watch themselves and to share with siblings and parents. At the end of the year, Ms. Haymes had a large collection of student-made videos teaching the social skills they had learned through the year.

Self-Management Strategies

Ms. Pauling and Ms. Haymes decide that the use of a schedule can help Emin to initiation of interactions towards peers. The written schedule for Emin lists activities for the day and for each activity there is a check for initiating towards peers. Emin is taught what appropriate initiations are through role playing and the use of video-modeling strategies. He is also taught to check off the initiation box on the schedule for each activity and then to tally the number of initiations that he made which can earn for him reinforcers, with a the more initiations he makes resulting in access to more highly desirable reinforcers.

Self-Determination

Making choices is an important component of being self-determined and Ms. Pauling understands that providing opportunities to engage first in simple, then increasingly complex choice making would be beneficial for Emin (Agran & Martin, 2014). Ms. Pauling understands that choice making in and of itself does not result in self-determination but that it is the beginning of the development of self-determination for Emin.

Emin needs help in expressing his preferences and appropriately making choices. In order to do this, Ms. Pauling sets up situations in which Emin's choices have two distinct components: (a) the identification of a preference, and (b) the act of communicating that preference. She does this mainly during transition times when students have a choice of settings and/or activities to do such as during free time. For instance, when going to the free play area, Ms. Haymes will give Emin a choice of three activities (two highly preferred and one less preferred so that he has to make a meaningful choice, not just an easy choice between a highly preferred or a less preferred activity which is not necessarily a meaningful choice that leads to self-determination). Ms. Haymes is also careful that Emin has opportunities to learn to make choices based on his own preferences but also to have activity experiences outside of his narrow range of highly preferred activities so that he is exposed to activities that may be of interest to him (but he won't know if they are or not until he experiences the activity).

Person-Centered Planning

Though Emin is young, Ms. Pauling encourages his family to have a Person-Centered Planning meeting so that everyone can have input into where Emin is currently and to look forward into the future regarding outcomes that will be important to he and his family.

Personal Profile Development: Ms. Pauling begins the meeting by assisting Emin's family members (mother and father, aunt and uncle, and grandmother) and the other important stakeholders (Mr. Barrios and Ms. Haymes) to construct a personal profile of Emin as recommended by Miner (2014). The personal profile is similar to a resume in that it describes the individual in terms of unique capabilities and capacities. Specific components of a personal profile include a circle of support map, community presence chart (which Ms. Pauling omits

due to Emin's age), preferences list, and a gifts and capacities description (Miner, 2014).

Circle of Support Map: The importance of relationships is evident in
the lives of most people. However, the importance of meaningful relationships is often underappreciated, and this is especially true for
Emin as this circle of support map shows how socially isolated Emin
is outside of his family. The map clearly shows that almost all of Emin's
social interactions are with adults and that he rarely interacts with
same-age peers and almost never has any play dates.

Developing a Preferences List: The team then develop a list of Emin's
preferences. It is striking to everyone how short the list is. This is an
obvious concern, especially since the preferences don't match at all
what same-age peers are interested in. In an effort to better understand Emin's preferences, the team delineates things that "work" and
"don't work" for Emin. This preference list establishes a much needed context for making decisions regarding Emin's support needs.

Expressing Gifts and Capacities: Emin has many gifts and capacities
such as his intelligence, his inquisitiveness, his caring about family
members, and his following routines, Emin's team appreciates seeing
this list as it helps them to focus on his positive attributes and this list
helps to increase the positive perspective expectations of a meaningful lifestyle for Emin.

Future Lifestyle Planning: This process develops a positive vision of
the future for Emin. Once the team has a positive vision of the future
(Emin will go to college, live in an apartment on his own or with a
roommate, have a job, and receive appropriate supports as necessary)
it is possible for them to plan on what needs to happen at least for the
next few years in elementary school to help Emin start on his way
towards this positive future.

Action Steps and Responsible Parties: Now that there is a vision for the
future, it is important that the team negotiate action steps and responsible parties. No personal profile or vision of the future is worthwhile
without action towards making the vision come true. The team
decides upon a few short-term tasks to start with (coordinating play
dates, involving Emin in a social skills group outside of school, and
working with the insurance company for Emin to receive in-home
Applied Behavior Analysis services.

Inclusion Outside of the Classroom in the School

The main places in the school for Emin to be included are the playground and the cafeteria. On the playground, Ms. Pauling and Ms. Haymes set up a system for students to encourage others to play with them in the "game of the day" (which rotates across different games that are popular with the students). They practice inviting others to join the game during class time and then again at the beginning of recess on the playground (since the kindergartners have their own recess time this is easy to do). As part of Emin's schedule he has to play with peers for at least one minute in the game of the day in order to earn a star for the recess time on his schedule. Ms. Haymes has a secret signal (putting her hands on her shoulders) to signal Emin when the one minute is up. Emin understands the contingency and is able to tolerate the one minute of play time with his peers in order to gain access to reinforcers.

In the cafeteria, Ms. Pauling involves Emin in a lunch buddies program where once a week he eats lunch with two second graders who have been taught by Ms. Pauling (following the recommendations by Müller and Cannon (2012) on how to have positive interactions with younger students:

a. select a topic for conversation
b. use information from on-topic questions or comments to formulate follow-up
c. questions and comments
d. use questioning strategies to elicit additional information and keep the conversation going
e. use attention gaining strategies to ensure that partners are listening use information known about a peer to select a conversation topic

Inclusion Outside of the School Setting

The information from the person-centered planning meeting has clearly shown everyone how isolated Emin is outside of the school setting. Emin's family decide to start in-home ABA services for him once they realize that these services can take place in the community (such as a playground or at playdates with same age peers) and thus these services are likely to result in his parents having better skills at helping him socially and in his being more included outside of school.

Executive Functioning

Emin has difficulty with executive functioning om the areas of emotional control and inhibiting impulses when unexpected changes to the schedule happen. Since he finds the use of written visual schedules to be helpful, Ms. Haymes decides to use a white board in where she writes down part of Emin's schedule and then adds in things like "fire drill," "earthquake drill," etc. She then goes over the schedule with Emin at the beginning of the day and they briefly discuss what to do if they occur and that they are unlikely to occur. When they do not occur, Ms. Haymes has Emin wipe off the words from the whiteboard. Once he is comfortable with this system, she sometimes adds it to his written schedule. This system provides antecedent opportunities for what may happen so that Emin is more prepared when they happen and thus able to establish emotional control in those situations.

Use of Technology

Emin enjoys the use of electronics and is skilled in their use that is appropriate for someone his age. He does like to watch videos and he responds well to videomodeling strategies which the staff are able to use in teaching him skills.

Physical, Medical, Psychological, or Mental Health Issues

Emin has good physical health. However, Emin's parents and the school staff are concerned that his lack of friends could cause mental health issues in the future and understand that helping him develop friends at an early age may be of great benefit to him as he becomes older.

Collaboration

Currently there is good collaboration between Emin's family and the school staff as well as among the school staff themselves. If other agencies become involved in supporting Emin (such as in-home ABA services) it will be important that there is collaboration with school staff so that interventions that are successful in one setting can potentially be implemented in other settings to increase generalization for Emin.

Legal Issues

Currently, there are no legal problems with Emin's programs. Emin's parents will need to decide if they want him to have an IEP or if the 504 services are providing enough support for him. If Emin does start receiving services outside of school, then his parents will need to be aware of any legal issues related to those services (such as those with insurance funding requirements for in-home ABA services.

Discussion Questions

1. Would Emin be better served in a class designed specifically for students with ASD as the staff there would have the training and expertise in this area?
2. Should peers be encouraged to interact with Emin? Shouldn't they have the choice of whom to interact with?
3. Should Emin have to interact with same age peers? Should he be allowed not to?
4. Would Emin benefit from having an IEP as well as a 504 Plan?
5. Would Emin benefit from being around peers who are like him (also academically gifted and also have ASD)?

References Cited in This Case Study

Agran, M., & Martin, J. (2014). Self-determination: Enhancing competence and independence. In K. Storey & D. Hunter, (Eds.), *The road ahead: Transition to adult life for persons with disabilities* (3rd ed., pp. 31–57). Washington, DC: IOS Press.

Attwood, T. (2008). *The complete guide to Asperger's Syndrome.* Philadelphia, PA: Jessica Kingsley Publisher.

Miner, C. (2014). Person-centered planning. In K. Storey & D. Hunter (Eds.), *The road ahead: Transition to adult life for persons with disabilities* (3rd ed., pp. 9–30). Washington, DC: IOS Press.

Müller, E., & Cannon, L. (2012). *Teaching conversation skills using the "lunch Buddies" program.* Rockville, MS: The Ivymount School.

O'Neill, R. E., Albin, R. W., Storey, K., Horner, R. H., & Sprague, J. R. (2015). *Functional assessment and program development for problem behavior: A practical handbook* (3rd ed.). Stamford, CT: Cengage Publishing Company.

CASE STUDY TWO: Ogodei

Case Study Covers:

- *Emotional Disturbance*
- *Elementary School*

Ogodei is a fifth-grade student who receives special education services under the Emotional Disturbance category. He was in a non-public school for students with disabilities the past four years. At that school the teachers spent much of their time dealing with challenging behaviors and Ogodei often imitated the behaviors that other students were engaging in (aggression, non-compliance, cursing, disruption to the class. elopement, etc.). Though he is intellectually quite bright, his academic performance is only fair as not a lot of academic instruction occurred at his previous school and he was a bit below grade when he started in Ms. Heig's class. His parents (and Ogodei as well), wanted to give him an opportunity in an inclusive setting to see how he would do. Ogadei currently receives a half hour of individual counseling per week from a counselor with the school district. He and his family also receive one hour of counseling services per week from a county mental health agency.

His teacher, Ms. Heig, is concerned that Ogodei does not take direction well from Ms. Heig (he is often defiant), that he yells out off-task and inappropriate phrases in class, and that he will sometimes become sullen and put his head down on his desk (Ms. Heig is concerned that he is depressed). It has been a struggle for Ogodei, his classmates, and his teacher. Just yesterday, Ms. Heig asked him to rewrite his story using the provided rubric, and Ogodei angrily replied that he didn't want to do anymore work on it, and then he stalked out of the room. This was not the first time an incident like this has happened where he was defiant at the teacher's request (this was a common student behavior at his previous school). In addition to these concerns about Ogodei's behavior, Ms. Heig had noticed that other students in the class are beginning to imitate Ogodei's defiant response to her requests. She wasn't sure of the cause for this behavior, but regardless of the cause, Ms. Heig decided that it was important to take immediate action and that the undesirable behavior should not be ignored.

On the plus side, Ogodei enjoys going to a "real school," does okay academically, and he follows a lot of the positive behaviors of his peers. He is starting to make some friends in class. Ms. Heig enjoys his sense of humor and he is often ready with a quip or joke in class. Outside of school Ogodei likes being physically active and he enjoys playing sports such as basketball, baseball, and soccer.

Accommodations

Ms. Heig makes two accommodations for Ogodei. The first is that she provides close proximity to her by having his desk in the front of the class. This makes it easier for her to monitor his behavior and to provide subtle verbal prompts to him if necessary. The second accommodation is that she makes a "calm area" in the back of the class with several bean bags on a rug area where Ogodei (and other students use it as well) can go do calm down or destress if they are feeling overwhelmed. She makes clear rules for the use of this area (they have to signal to Ms. Heig that they are going there, no more than 5 minutes, students have to be quiet, no distracting others) so that students are not using it to escape from tasks.

Modifications

Ms. Heig makes several modifications in order to support Ogodei (as well as several other students in her class). First, she adapts the number of items that Ogodei is expected to complete. This includes a reduction in the length of written reports and the number of problems to be solved during math work. This allows Ogodei to be successful in his initial work and also allows Ms. Heig to then slowly increase the work expectation for Ogodei. Ms. Heig also modifies the way that instruction is delivered to Ogodei (as well with other students) as she sees that he does much better with concrete examples that include hands-on activities.

Instructional Strategies

There is a logical connection between Ogodei's academic performance and his need for positive behavior supports. Ms.Heig understands that often challenging behaviors and escape behaviors occur because the student is avoiding academic situations in which they do not have the academic skills to succeed. So she is careful to analyze Ogodei's behaviors from an academic standpoint. For instance, since Ogodei's reading skills are poor, if he is asked to read a passage out loud it is difficult for him and also he is afraid to look foolish and incompetent in front of his peers, he then is likely to mouth off to Ms. Heig in order to avoid embarrassment.

Ms. Heig decides upon a variety of instructional strategies to help Ogodei. First, she gives him a "choice" in selecting stories to read, and having less vocabulary words to learn than his peers. Ms. Heig also spends 5 minutes of direct individual instruction time each day with Ogodei and two other students who also need more instruction on reading. Ms. Heig also decides to use a behavioral contract stating that for each 20 minutes of working, Ogodei receives the option of a "fun break." Ms. Heig teaches Ogodei how to keep track of the twenty minutes on-task with a card on his desk. It was also agreed that between the two of them that Ms. Heig will send a weekly progress email to Ogodei parents and Ogodei receives a star on his contract for successful work each day. In addition, Ms. Heig knew that it was important to build Ogodei's sight vocabulary and recognizing syllables (Jennings, Caldwell, & Lerner, 2014). So Ms. Heig combines Interventions of repeated reading, read-along, paired reading, and echo reading for increasing Ogodei's vocabulary (Lerner & Johns, 2015). Ms. Heig also uses modeling, guided practice, independent practice, and corrective feedback for teaching Ogodei vocabulary words (Edmonds, et al., 2009). In this way, Ms. Heig combines solid teaching strategies with positive behavior supports strategies.

Supports for Teachers

Ms. Heig feels well supported with the assistance that she receives from Mr. Sugai (the coordinator for the School Wide Positive Behavior Supports (SWPBS) program for the school), and Ms. Haruko (vice-principal of the school). Ms. Heig, Mr. Sugai, and Ms. Haruko make sure that other teachers and staff (including office staff, recess monitors, and lunch monitors) that work with Ogodei receive information about him and support strategies that are effective (praising him when he is following the rules) and also strategies that are not effective (yelling at him for doing things wrong). Ms. Haruko has weekly check-ins with these staff to discuss students that need extra support so that any issues that arise are dealt with quickly and positively.

Support for Peers

Ms. Heig recognizes that peers are starting to sometimes imitate Ogodei's challenging behaviors and she decides upon an indirect and positive strategy to decrease this imitation. As part of her curriculum across different areas (science, history, etc.) she makes sure that she includes a part on positive role models. She discusses role models across ethnic, cultural, gender, economic, and other areas. During circle time she adds in a section where students can talk about role models in their own lives. Ms. Heig includes discussions of behaviors that make someone a positive role model or not a positive role model. Ms. Heig hopes that these discussions will assist students in analyzing that imitating Ogodei's behavior is not a good idea and also provide Ogodei with positive role models as well.

Support for Family

Ogodei's parents are currently receiving counseling and mental health services for themselves as well as for parenting Ogodei. His parents have asked that communication from Ms. Heig be on a daily basis if possible and that it includes a positive component of something good that Ogodei did that day so that there is a basis for reinforcing him at home for that behavior and that the news is not always bad.

Positive Behavior Supports

School-Wide Positive Behavior Supports: Unfortunately, Ogodei has received quite a few office referrals (the office makes sure to send a copy of each office referral home) so Mr. Sugai flagged the number of office referrals for Ogodei and brought this information to the SWPBS team. It was decided at this meeting to pursue a more intensive individualized intervention to correct Ogodei's disruptive and noncompliant behaviors. The SWPBS team meets with Ogodei, his parents, and

Ms. Heig. The team recommends that Ogodei participate in the Behavior Education Program (BEP), where a daily progress report gets home for his parents to sign. Ogodei checks in with the school's BEP coordinator when he arrived at school and takes the daily progress report to his teacher, who records her data during the day. At the end of the day, Ogodei retrieves the progress report from the teacher and returns it to the BEP coordination for a reward (if it is a good report). A copy of the BEP is then made for Ogodei to take home for his parent's signature. Ogodei then returns the progress report to the BEP coordinator the next morning, and the cycle continues with Ogodei given a new daily progress report.

Functions of Behavior: Mr. Sugai's assessment indicates that the primary function of Ogodei's behavior is to escape from academic demands or other non-preferred activities.

Skill Building: Mr. Sugai uses the Aggression Replacement Training program (Goldstein, Glick, & Gibbs, 1986) with a group of students and he adds Ogodei to this group. ART teaches alternative skills to anger and aggression and the three components of ART are:

A: SkillStreaming, which teaches a curriculum of ProSocial, interpersonal skills (i.e., what to do instead of aggression).

B: Anger Control Training (ACT), which teaches students what to do, as well as what not to do, if provoked. The goal of ACT is to teach students self-control of anger. Mr. Sugai has students bring to each session a description of a recent anger-arousing experience that they record in a binder. For ten sessions, the students receive instruction from Mr. Sugai in responding to their frustrations with a chain of behaviors that include:

  1. Identifying triggers (i.e., those external events and internal self-statements that provoke an anger response, such as being too close to a particular peer or having one's space suddenly invaded).

  2. Identifying cues (i.e., those individual physical events, such as tightened muscles, flushed faces, and clenched fists, which let the student know that the emotion he or she is experiencing is anger).

  3. Using reminders (i.e., self-statements, such as "stay calm," "chill out," and "cool down," or non-hostile explanations of others' behavior).

4. Using reducers (i.e., a series of techniques that, like the use of reminders, is designed expressly to lower the student's level of anger, such as deep breathing, counting backward, imagining a peaceful scene, or imagining the long-term consequences of one's behavior).
5. Using self-evaluation (i.e., reflecting on how well the frustration was responded to by identifying triggers, identifying cues, using reminders, and using reducers and then praising or rewarding oneself for effective performance).

C: Moral Reasoning Training, which promotes values that respect the rights of others and helps students to want to use the interpersonal and anger management skills taught. The goal of moral reasoning training is to have students think about moral issues from different perspectives and examine their judgments, as well as those of others. Mr. Sugai uses group meetings where relevant examples of moral dilemmas are presented. In these meetings, each student in the group is asked to describe the proper behavior the person in the dilemma should do, and why.

Reinforcement: Ms. Heig, Mr. Sugai, and Ogodei also agreed on prompts (a special hand signal the teacher would use) to remind to not shout out. Ogodei then receives a prize from the class prize box on the days he had "no shoutouts."

Social Supports

Ogodei generally does okay in social situations outside of the classroom as peers appreciate his sense of humor and his ability to tell jokes. However, Ms. Haruko makes sure that the recess and lunch monitors keep a close eye on Ogodei as these are times when students are sometimes not under close supervision and things can go wrong. Ms. Haruko keeps close track of what is going on during these times and that the monitors are close to Ogodei or at least have him in their sight and that they are providing praise for this positive interactions with peers and for his following the rules (such as lining up correctly when returning to class).

Social Skills Instruction

In order to help Ogodei with classroom situations that are difficult for him, Ms. Heig locates a lesson from the Skillstreaming program on Responding to Difficult Requests (McGinnis, 2012). She includes a role-play for "responding to teacher requests" into the lesson scenarios (Ogodei was not the only student who sometimes had difficulty responding appropriately to teacher requests). The Skillstreaming lesson is included in the social studies period right after lunch break and the students enjoy the active role-plays. Initially, after having students provide examples of difficult requests (luckily one example included a teacher asking a student to do an assignment over), Ms. Heig modeled the steps to use for responding. These steps were: (a) listen to what the other person is requesting, (b) restate back what you understand the person is asking, (c) if you disagree, ask the other person to explain anything you don't agree with, (d) if you still disagree, politely provide the person with the information and reason you feel or think differently, and (e) stop and think about the person's response and the best way to handle the situation. Ms. Heig guided students through the role-plays (making sure to include Ogodei) and provided immediate corrections if steps were missed. The next day, Ms. Heig took advantage of "teachable moments" when students could be reminded to use this new skill in responding to difficult requests throughout the school day, and she provided the students with praise. On Friday, she gave the students a ten-minute popcorn break at the end of the day for their excellence in responding to her requests.

Self-Management Strategies

Mr. Sugai and Ms. Heig put into place a self-management system that has these components:

Self-management used to reduce agitation: Ms. Heig and Mr. Sugai feel that Ogodei would find it useful to have a list of steps to follow when he is angry or upset. To help in these situations. Ogodei keeps a card at his desk to pull out and read to help him reduce the agitation. For the use of the cards, Mr. Sugai teaches Ogodei to use self-verbalization and self-monitoring in upsetting academic/social situations to help him from losing self-control and responding impulsively. On the card Ogodei has previously written questions to help him "stop and think" before responding.

Self-monitoring and self-recording: This involves Ogodei evaluating whether he has performed a behavior (self-monitoring) along with creating a written record of each time the behavior is performed (self-recording). In this process, the self-monitoring provides the opportunity for Ogodei to become aware of his performance (when he is performing the positive behavior as well as when he is not performing the positive behavior). Ogodei finds it useful to keep frequency counts of when he successfully calmed himself during difficult situations.

Self-Determination

Ms. Heig and Mr. Sugai are careful to ask Ogodei what he wants to involve him in the development of supports and interventions as much as possible. This often involves informal talks with Ogodei for short time periods during lunch or recess or "special time" with one of them in a neutral place in the school such as the recess area while shooting baskets. Ms. Heig and Mr. Sugai talk with Ogodei about the situations and his behaviors and then outline a possible intervention (such as the self-management system) or give him choices (such as what type of self-management system to use after explaining and demonstrating several different ones). This helps to get Ogodei's buy-in and also assists him in becoming self-determined.

Person-Centered Planning

Ms. Haruko expresses her concerns about Ogodei's behavior to his parents and recommends that the team have a person-centered planning meeting. After she explains to the parents what this meeting would entail and why it would be beneficial they agree to have a Person-Centered Planning meeting and at the meeting these components were covered:

Personal Profile Development: Mr. Sugai facilitates the person-centered planning meeting (Ms. Heig is also there). The meeting starts with Ogodei's parents constructing a personal profile of Ogodei with Mr. Sugai's assistance, as recommended by Miner (2014).

Circle of Support Map: This analysis indicates that though Ogodei has social interactions with peers due to his involvement in sports, these are not necessarily sustained or important social networks for him. This visual information also provides feedback to his parents as they then also have an increased understanding that they also have a very small social network themselves.

Developing a preferences list: The team develops a list of Ogodei's preferences. The list mainly involves sports activities. In delineating things that "work" and "don't work" for Ogodei they see that physical activity and sports work for him while sitting for extended time periods or spending time with others outside of sports doesn't work for him.

Expressing gifts and capacities: Ogodei's gifts and capacities such include his sense of humor, being in good physical shape, and enjoying physical activities and sports. He is also close to his parents and is concerned about their welfare and mental health as well as his own issues in these areas.

Future Lifestyle Planning: This process helps to develop a positive vision of the future for Ogodei. His parents see Ogodei graduating from high school and starting work and maybe going to a community college as well. Because of his interest in physical activity and sports the team sees these possible career areas for him.

Action Steps and Responsible Parties: With this vision for the future, Mr. Sugai goes over the importance of *action steps and responsible parties.* This makes it more likely that the vision will come true. The team decides upon a some initial tasks to start with (encouraging get-togethers with team mates from sports teams, forming a group of peers for physical activities outside of sports, and making sure that his parents are receiving mental health services themselves as well as taking parent skills classes through their health insurance.

Inclusion Outside of the Classroom in the School

Ogodei is pretty well included during recess and lunch time when he generally plays basketball or soccer with other students. Sometimes when he is depressed the lunch and recess staff need to encourage him to play basketball or soccer with peers. Usually he does so but sometimes he says that he wants to be alone and the staff respect his choice and do not force the issue with him.

Outside of the School Inclusion Setting

Currently Ogodei is well included outside of school in his different sports activities. This is not a concern at this point in time.

Executive Functioning

In regards to executive functioning skills, Ogodei is strong in initiating some activities such as playing sports with peers in the neighborhood. He struggles with executive functioning areas of shifting attemtion, emotional control, and inhibiting impulses.

For shifting attention, if Ogodei likes an activity, he is able to focus on it for extended time periods. If he does not like an activity, he has a very short attention span and after a short time on that task is likely to start engaging in challenging behaviors.

In regard to inhibiting impulses and emotional control, Ogodei often lacks the ability to control his impulses and to stop his challenging behaviors when he wants to avoid tasks or to get attention. Ms. Heig consults with Mr. Sugai and they decide upon the use of an antecedent procedure involving the manipulation of motivating operations which is teaching him to clasp his hands and count to five when he wants to avoid a task which builds in a short blocking response before engaging in the challenging behavior which helps to build a short window of time for an intervention. Mr. Sugai suggests a package of components of self-instruction including verbal pre-testing, contingent reinforcement, multiple exemplars, reminders to use self-instructional statements in performance, and self-reinforcement (Hughes & Agran, 1994).

Use of Technology

Since Ogodei is behind academically, especially with reading and since he is fairly technologically savvy, Ms. Heig works with him on the use of different technology supports for reading such as the use of visual tools such as automatic scaffolding and layer concept maps (Yang, 2015), the use of wikis (Lenz, 2014), or a web-based reading annotation system with an attention-based self-regulated learning mechanism (ASRLM) (Chen & Huang, 2014). Ogodei finds these tools useful in that he can use them at school and also at home. It is helpful for Ogodei in that he can access the modules as much as he needs to and at home it is private so peers do not see him struggling at school.

Collaboration

Ms. Haruko also coordinates services with agencies that provide services to students who attend the school (either at the school, at community sites, or in their home setting). Ms. Haruko and the other agencies use Wraparound services as a team-based planning process to providing community-based care for students with complex mental health and related issues. The teams include the student, family members, service providers, and members of the family's social support network. Wraparound services are not a specific intervention or service and the purpose of the wraparound process is to bring together the student and the family with needed supports, such as medical coordinators, family and youth peer-to-peer support partners, mental health workers, social workers, and so on to develop comprehensive interventions (rather than piecemeal approaches from each individual or agency) to meet the needs of the student, the family, and others. Wraparound services are not based on any single theory of intervention; wraparound is best understood as a planning process and a philosophy of care (Eber, Hyde, & Suter, 2011). Ms. Haruko coordinates services for Ogodei using the four distinct phases outlined by Walker (2008). First, she focuses on engagement and team development and since she is the Wraparound facilitator she meets with Ogodei and his parents to engage them in the process, address concerns, explain how this process is different from traditional interventions, and help the family decide who they want on their Wraparound team. The second phase involves the initial plan development and Ms. Haruko gets the parents and team together and helps them to reach consensus and buy in on the desired outcomes. Ms. Haruko is careful that both Ogodei needs and strengths are used to identify specific interventions as well as to clarify roles for all team members. For phase three Ms. Haruko focuses on plan implementation which focuses on effectively meet the needs of the Ogodei by combining supports such as peer mentoring, counseling, specialized academic instruction (such as for reading), and addressing medical issues. Ms. Haruko also makes sure that supports for his parents are available such as mental health counseling services and are being utilized. Finally, Ms. Haruko looks ahead to plan completion and transition where Ogodei and his parents are eventually transitioned to less intensive structures, such as parent-teacher conference or agency contacts.

Legal Issues

Since Ogodei's and his parents are receiving support from a number of agencies it will be important that information only be shared between agencies and the school with the formal approval of his parents. Ogodei's parents will need to be aware of different requirements and services among the school and different agencies.

Discussion Questions

1. Should students with emotional, behavioral, and mental health issues be educated in special counseling enriched settings or are they better served in inclusive environments?
2. Is it realistic for students with serious challenging behaviors to move directly from a non-public school into an inclusion class?
3. Should so much support, both at school and in home, be given to only one student? Would it be better if services were spread out among other students as well?

References Cited in This Case Study

Chen, C. M., & Huang, S. H. (2014). Web-based reading annotation system with an attention-based self-regulated learning mechanism for promoting reading performance. *British Journal of Educational Technology, 45,* 959–980.

Eber, L., Hyde, K., & Suter, J. (2011). Integrating wraparound into a schoolwide system of positive behavior supports. *Journal of Child and Family Studies, 20,* 782–790.

Edmonds, M. S., Vaughn, S., Wexler, J., Reutebuch, C., Cable, A., Tackett, K. K., & Schnakenberg, J. W. (2009). A synthesis of reading interventions and effects on reading comprehension outcomes for older struggling students. *Review of Educational Research, 79,* 262–300.

Goldstein, A. P., Glick, B., & Gibbs, J. (1986). *Aggression replacement training: A comprehensive intervention for aggressive youth.* Champaign, IL: Research Press.

Hughes, C., & Agran, M. (1994). Teaching persons with severe disabilities to use self-instruction in community settings: An analysis of applications. *Journal of the Association for Persons with Severe Handicaps, 18,* 261–274.

Jennings, J. H., Caldwell, J. S., Lerner, J. W. (2014). *Reading problems: Assessment and teaching strategies* (7th ed.). Boston, MA: Pearson.

Lenz, C. (2014). Can we talk? A model for active reading comprehension using technology. *Journal of Adolescent and Adult Literacy, 58,* 109–109.

Lerner, J. W., & Johns, B. H. (2015). *Learning disabilities and related disabilities: Strategies for success* (13th ed.). Stamford, CT: Cengage.

McGinnis, E. (2012). *Skillstreaming the elementary school child: A guide for teaching prosocial skills* (3rd ed.). Champaign, IL, US: Research Press.

Miner, C. (2014). Person-centered planning. In K. Storey & D. Hunter (Eds.), *The road ahead: Transition to adult life for persons with disabilities* (3rd ed., pp. 9–30). Washington, DC: IOS Press.

Walker, J. S. (2008). *How, and why, does wraparound work: A theory of change.* Portland, OR: National Wraparound Initiative, Portland State University.

Yang, Y. F. (2015). Automatic scaffolding and measurement of concept mapping for EFL students to write summaries. *Journal of Educational Technology and Society, 18,* 273–286.

CASE STUDY THREE: Della

Case Study Covers:

- *Multiple Disabilities*
- *Middle School*

Della is 13 years old and in seventh grade. It is her first year in middle school. She is diagnosed as having multiple disabilities which for her includes an intellectual disability, an orthopedic impairment, epilepsy (Tonic-clonic or grand mal seizures where her body stiffens, jerks, and shakes, and Della can lose consciousness), and challenging behaviors (yelling, throwing things, and laying on the floor). Della uses a walker to assist her in moving around the classroom and her school. Sometimes she will use a wheelchair if she needs to travel long distances such as when she is on a field trip or if she is tired after having a seizure. A one-to-one aide, Ms. Slenker, is with Della throughout the school day to help support her socially and academically as well as with her physical needs (such as toileting and eating) and to assist her in case she has a seizure.

Della comes from a large and loving family where she is the fourth of five children. Both of her parents have college degrees and professional careers. There is an au pair who lives with the family and helps with Della in the morning and after school. Her siblings also assist in supporting Della as well. Della is involved with her family outside of school as the family enjoys going to music events, museums, and restaurants. Della participates in these activities with her family and her siblings often include her in their social activities as well.

In school Della is outgoing and enjoys interacting with peers and adults though sometimes her speech can be difficult to understand. She does not like to sit for long periods of time and will sometimes engage in challenging behaviors when this happens. Academically, Della has a modified curriculum though she spends most of her day in the general education classes. Ms. Garff is the inclusion specialist for the middle school and she provides support to the teachers and peers as well as to Della and her aide.

Accommodations

It will be important to Ms. Garff to monitor the teaching time that Della is receiving on academic instruction. After a certain amount of teaching time and trying different strategies it a decision will have to be made whether Della is going to learn the academic skills or not and if modifications, and accommodations may be necessary and appropriate. If Della is not learning academic skills at an acceptable rate, then the team will need to consider alternatives to those skills that lead to the desirable outcome (such as not being able to tell time but having the outcome of knowing what time it is for following a picture schedule). This is known as a multilevel activity where Della participates in activity but learns at different levels (some expressive others receptive). Ms. Garff also sets up academic instruction where Della participates in curriculum overlap activities where she participates in the same activity as her peers but works on different target skills (such as having social interactions in group cooperative learning situations).

Brown, Schwarz, Udvari-Solner, Kampschroer, Johnson, Jorgensen, and Gruenewald (1991) address the complexity of the analysis and decisions to be made ("sacrifices, trades, and compromises") regarding the inclusion of students with severe disabilities. Ayres, Lowrey, Douglas, and Sievers (2011) and Courtade, Spooner, Browder, and Jimenez (2012) provide pros and cons and guidelines on these complex issues that Ms. Garff and the team read these articles and have two brief group discussions about them and all find benefit in reading and discussing these articles with fellow teachers.

While in school, it is important that her teachers and family understand that Della will benefit from learning functional skills that relate to the Criterion of Ultimate Functioning (Brown, Nietupski, & Hamre-Nietupski, 1976). The criterion of ultimate functioning refers to referencing skills that the student will need as an adult. For example, for Della these skills could include being independent taking care of personal hygiene, dressing independently, and having appropriate travel skills. With the consideration of the Criterion of Ultimate Functioning many academic skills are of doubtful value in order to function as an adult in society. Ms. Garff is careful to have goals that relate specifically to the criterion of ultimate functioning in her IEP.

Modifications

Ms. Garff and Della's teachers understand that Della will need to have her academic curriculum modified for her to be successfully included in her classes. They decide upon a variety of strategies:

Quantity: Adapt the number of items that Della is expected to learn or complete. For example, in social studies class Della is expected to learn a reduced number of terms than her peers.

Input: Adapt the way instruction is delivered to Della. In math class, more concrete examples (such as number of items to manipulate rather than completing written math problems).

Difficulty: Adapt the rules for Della. In math class, Della uses a calculator for some problems.

Output: Adapt how Della can respond to instruction. For oral presentations, Della is allowed to pre-program a communication device with voice output.

Alternative Goals: Adaptations are made for Della's outcome expectations. In social studies Della locates colors on map while other students identify countries.

Substitute Curriculum: Della is often provided with different instruction and materials. At some times when academic classroom instruction is happening for other students, Della is learning how to use her communication device in the speech language room with her speech pathologist.

Even if Della cannot complete all parts of tasks or activities at school, she is able to partially participate. Partial participation means that students who might not have or not be able to acquire all of the skills needed to completely participate in activities are still capable of learning enough skills to partially participate (Baumgart, Brown, Pumpian, Nisbet, Ford, Sweet, Messina, & Schroeder, 1982; Ferguson & Baumgart, 1991). Doyle and Giangreco (2013) state that "Partial participation offers a constructive alternative to an "all or nothing" mentality that too often leads to students with intellectual disabilities being separated from the general education classroom, curriculum, and nondisabled peers" (p. 63). Thus, Ms. Garff needs to make it clear to others (teachers, staff, and peers) that the expectation is that Della is an active participant in activities even if she is partially participating. That she should not be a passive participant.

Ms. Garff uses the four components of partial participation as outlined by Ferguson and Baumgart to assist in including Della:

Utilizing/creating materials and devices. These adaptations refer to portable objects, equipment, or materials created for instructional purposes that enhance or allow partial participation. For example, in the cooking class, though Della cannot independently make a smoothie, she can hit an electronic switch with her hand to activate the blender.

Utilizing personal assistance. This refers to cues or supervisory assistance provided by another person. For example, Della could have a school office job where she is capable of shredding documents correctly when at the shredder but needs assistance in locating materials that are to be shredded.

Adapting skills sequences. This involves using a sequence that is different from that used by most individuals without disabilities. For instance, carrying a loaded tray of food in a cafeteria is difficult for Della, but making multiple trips (one for silverware, one for food, one for a drink) may allow her to be able to independently complete the task of getting her food to a table.

Adapting rules. Rules are prescribed guidelines, procedures, or customs for engaging in activities. An example of adapting rules is provided by Bernabe and Block (1994) who helped to include a 12-year-old female with moderate/severe disabilities in a softball league. One adaptation that was made for her was that she was allowed to hit off a tee rather than from a pitched ball. This strategy could be used for Della as well in her physical education class.

Instructional Strategies

Della often has difficulty on picking up on the cue (discriminative stimulus) in the environment for what she is to do. Ms. Garff understands that instructors often mistakenly think that the purpose of instruction is to get the person to do what they prompted to do. However, Ms. Garff understands that the real purpose of instruction is to get the learner to respond appropriately to the natural stimuli in the environment so that they can perform skills independently. For example, when the teacher in Della's class says it is time to put your materials away and get ready for the bell Ms. Slenker could verbally prompt Della to put her materials away but in that case Della is responding to Ms. Slenker rather than her teacher. Instead Ms. Slenker could give an indirect verbal cue that is related to the cue in the environment such as "what did the teacher tell everyone to do" or "what are others in the class doing now?" these are cue that highlights the discriminative stimulus from the teacher. Thus, the indirect verbal prompt from Ms. Slenker is giving Della information so that she can perform the behavior when it is appropriate to do so.

Task analysis: A task analysis is a process of breaking a task into its required component responses and listing these responses in an appropriate sequence (Bellamy, Horner, & Inman, 1979). In other words, it is a complete description of each and every behavior needed to accomplish a specific activity. The purpose of task analysis is to facilitate instruction by focusing the instructor's attention on the specific demands of a task and by providing a method for gathering data during instruction about the acquisition of the task by the learner. The teaching of complex tasks proceeds most efficiently if the tasks are shaped by successive approximations. People learn simpler component responses and chain them together ultimately to perform the complex target behavior (Cuvo, 1978). Ms. Garff develops task analyses for activities that are important for Della to learn in school. One task that Della has been working on at school is how to wash her hands and Ms. Garff develops a task analysis for Ms. Slenker to use for instructional purposes. Figure 3.1 provides the task analysis that is being used.

Chaining Method: Ms. Garff and Ms. Slenker decide to use backward chaining procedures for teaching Della how to wash her hands as well as other self-care skills. With backward chaining, the last

Figure 3.1 Task Analysis for Handwashing.

- Put one hand under spout of soap dispenser.
- With other hand push top of soap dispenser so that soap comes out.
- With non-soap hand turn on cold water faucet.
- Wet both hands.
- Rub hands together for 15 seconds so that both hands are completely covered in soap.
- Continue to rub hands together until they are both free of soap.
- Turn off cold water faucet.
- Get paper towel.
- Wipe hands with paper towel until both are dry.
- Put towel into trash.

response in the task analysis is taught first, then the response that precedes it, and so on until the first response in the sequence is taught. The advantage of backward chaining is that the response closest to the terminal reinforcer is taught first (Storey & Minter, 2017).

Greatest to Least Prompts: Because of Della's difficulty in understanding discriminative stimuli and in learning new skills, Ms. Garff decides to use a system of greatest to least prompts to teach her skills using task analyses. In most-to-least prompting, the instructor begins by providing the most amount of assistance during initial instructional session and then systematically decreases the amount of assistance across sessions (e.g., starting with full physical guidance, then partial physical, then gesture, then verbal direction, and then allowing opportunity) until a criterion of correct independent responses is reached (Collins, Lo, Park, & Haughney, 2018). This method of instruction allows Della to learn tasks with minimal chances for errors.

Supports for Teacher

Della is new to the school and her teachers. Early in the year is becomes clear to Ms. Garff that Della's teachers see Della as Ms. Slenker's responsibility and pretty much ignore Della. It is also obvious to Ms. Garff that Ms. Slenker is unsure what her role is and is not effective in providing support and instruction to Della. Though it would be easy to blame the teachers for their lack of involvement with Della, Ms. Garff understands that Della's teachers need information about Della and her disabilities as well as strategies for supporting her in their classes. Ms. Garff also decides to provide information on her role as well as the role for Ms. Slenker. Ms. Garff makes a one page "cheat sheet" for the teachers providing basic information on Della and her disabilities, what her IEP goals are, as well as some bullet points on how to best teach Della, and Ms. Garff also includes some positive points regarding contributions that Della can make to the class and how modified instruction and universal design procedures can help other students as well. Ms. Garff also creates another one page "cheat sheet" regarding her role and Ms. Slenker's role (what we do and what we don't do). Ms. Garff sets up a brief 15-minute meeting with each teacher during their prep period or after school and makes sure to ask the teachers what she can do to support them as well as Della.

Ms. Garff creates a "cheat sheet" for Ms. Slenker as well that covers Della's IEP goals, expectations for what Della should do during classes, bullet points for instruction and handling behavioral issues. Ms. Garff knows that just giving Ms. Slenker written information is not enough so she is sure to spend time with Della and Ms. Slenker where she talks through what is in the "cheat sheet" and also models how to support Della, engages in role playing where they both take turns being Della, and she then provides Ms. Slenker with feedback and reinforcement for when she is working with Della.

Support for Peers

While some of the students at the school know Della many do not and they have not encountered a peer like her in their elementary education. With the help of Della and her family, Ms. Garff prepares a brief presentation about Della, information about what a disability is, and why inclusion is important to Della as well as to them. Della and Ms. Garff then make the presentation to the different classes that Della is in and then take questions from the students. There are a lot of questions and after the presentation Della's peers have more understanding and Della and her behaviors as well as how Della is different but also same as they are. Finally, to help support all students in the school and to create more positive attitudes, Ms. Garff incorporated "Ability Awareness" components as part of multi-cultural events at the school (Lindsay & Edwards, 2013).

Support for Family

Della's family members understand what inclusion is and also that inclusion for Della may look different in middle school than it did in elementary school. It will be important for Ms. Garff to provide information about what is going on in Della's classes both academically and socially to her family. In addition, the family will benefit receiving information about inclusion opportunities such as clubs and social events at the school so that the family members and Ms. Garff can discuss and coordinate supports for Della at these events.

Positive Behavior Supports

Della's challenging behaviors of yelling, throwing things, and laying on the floor are concerning for her ability to function in inclusive environments and also because they disrupt the learning of the other students in the classes. Ms. Garff and Della's teachers realize that reducing or eliminating these behaviors is important and they consult with the district behavior specialist, Ms. Dauster, who agrees that these behaviors need an intervention as quickly as possible. Ms. Dauster uses the Functional Assessment Interview Form (FAIF) and the Functional Assessment Observation Form (FAOF) from O'Neill, Albin, Storey, Horner, and Sprague (2015). The FAIF assists in identifying target behaviors, alternative replacement behaviors, setting events commonly associated with incidences of undesirable behavior, and observed social and environmental consequences of behaviors. The primary purpose of interview data is to begin to develop hypotheses about the functions of undesirable behavior being exhibited by Della.

The FAOF was used as a continuous measurement procedure recording the occurrence of yelling, throwing things, and laying on the floor across the entire school day. Use of the FAOF allows the team to collect direct observation data that analyzes the time frames in which data collection occurred (in this example it is different class sessions), what the undesirable behaviors are, the predictors (e.g., antecedents) for the behavior, the perceived function of the behavior (get/obtain or escape/avoid), and the consequences of the behaviors.

The results from the FAOF and FAI indicate that the function of Della's laying on the floor is to avoid tasks that she does not like or when she has been sitting too long (escape behaviors). The function of the yelling and throwing things is to get attention from peers and staff.

Ms. Dauster understands that since the function of Della's undesirable behavior of yelling and throwing things is to obtain attention that an alternative behavior that serves the same function is to teach Della appropriate ways of obtaining attention. Directly teaching Della social initiation skills towards peers and adults is a logical replacement behavior so that Della is not dependent upon others to initiate interactions (Owen-DeSchryver, Carr, Cale, & Blakeley-Smith, 2008). Ms. Dauster and Ms. Garr understand that for teaching social interactions skills it is best to use a combination of strategies that include modeling, role playing, and feedback (Storey, 2002). It will be important that social skills instruction consider the contextual variables of the environment as they relate to social initiations so that Della's initiations do not interrupt on-task behaviors or academic task completion by peers.

For Della's escape behavior of laying on the floor the functional alternative behavior Ms. Dauster decides to teach her to ask for a break. When Della asks for a break initially, she is immediately given one (so that she understands the relationship between her asking and then obtaining the break). After a week of this intervention, Ms. Garff and Ms. Dauster agree that Della understands the connection and then they require Della to complete a very short task before the break. Then there is a gradual increase in the amount of work that Della has to complete over time (Kreibich, Chen., & Reichle, 2015). For the laying on floor and throwing items, the team usees a Differential Reinforcement of Other Behavior (DRO) intervention where Ms. Slenker praises Della every five minutes in which no instances of yelling, throwing, or laying on the floor occurred which reinforces the absence of these behaviors and also provides additional positive interactions for Della.

Social Supports

Ms. Garff understands that critical social times in middle school are during lunch and times students are on the quad and decides that the use of peer buddies in lunch room and on the quad would likely an effective way to help support Della socially. She also understands that Della's having a 1:1 aide could get in the way of social interactions between Della and her non-disabled peers while the peer buddies can help facilitate Della's social interactions and increase her social standing with non-disabled peers. Ms. Garff is careful to follow the guidelines provided by Copeland et al. (2002) in setting up the peer buddy program for Della. First, she thoroughly screen peers Making sure that they have good social standing in the school) and she does not include the two students from the cooking club so that even more peers are engaged in supporting Della, second, she establish clear expectations for peers (that they are there to help Della socially and focus on her being socially included), and third she models and teaches expectations for the peers (they spend time with Della and Ms. Garff where Ms. Garff shows how Della uses her communication device and how to prompt and model behaviors for Della).

Social Skills Instruction

As noted above, teaching social initial skills to Della is an important intervention that is likely to have an important impact in her life across many different settings. In addition, teaching Della how to use an attention seeking card (one that has a picture of two people interacting and the words "I would like your attention please") would be an easy method for Della to gain attention appropriately.

Self-Management Strategies

Della understands what a social initiation is, so event recording for her social initiations would is a logical self-management strategy to implement. Ms. Garff decides upon a strategy where every time Della initiates a social interaction she moves a coin from her left pocket to her right pocket. This helps to provide visual feedback to Della (and others) on how well she did each day. This self-monitoring will provide an opportunity for Della the to become better aware of her performance and also provide feedback to her and others on how well she is doing.

Self-Advocacy

Ms. Garff understands that like all of us, Della will benefit from learning self-advocacy skills. However, Della's severity of disability makes it difficult for her to understand abstract constructs such as self-advocacy. Della currently does not have self-advocacy skills and her family members are her most important advocates. Ms. Garff consults with Della's family on this issue and they come up with two strategies to start with.

The first is through a service learning program at the local high school, Della is connected with a self-advocacy mentor, Allison, who also has a disability. Allison has received training on advocacy from the local Center for Independent Living and she spends time with Della and her family and also visits Della at school. Allison is then available to help Della in meeting with Ms. Garff and Della's teachers, attend meetings, and generally be there to assist Della in advocating for herself.

The second strategy is teaching Della more socially acceptable ways to express her wants and needs. Ms. Garff and Ms. Dauster teach Della how to say "I need a break" on her Assisted Communication device in situations associated with escape-motivated behavior. Thus, Della is more able to use antecedent and positive skills to communicate her needs.

Self-Determination

Part of being self-determined is the ability to express preferences and to make choices (Agran & Martin, 2014). It will be important to provide Della with meaningful as well as a wide range of choices so that she is able to make informed choices through exposure to settings, situations, and people with appropriate supports. For example, it would not be an informed and supported choice if Della goes to the cooking club after school one time and then making a subjective judgment if she liked it or not. However, analyzing skills and supports ahead of time by having Ms. Garff observe the club, pre-teaching expectations and skills to Della, providing information and suggestions for supporting Della to peers in the club, having an aide with Della during three visits would provide more experience and information in which to make a judgment if Della liked the club and if it would appear to be a good match for her.

Person-Centered Planning

Person-centered planning would be a productive way to encourages a positive view of Della's future based on her strengths and preferences rather than upon her deficits (Miner & Bates, 1997). For Della, the process of person centered planning should consist of four components: (1) a personal profile that promotes a positive view of the individual, (2) a challenging vision of the future, (3) action steps leading to the attainment of the desirable future lifestyle, and (4) any necessary changes to the current support system (i.e., school services or services outside of school).

Della is approaching her transition to high school and it may be beneficial to have an informal PCP meeting while she is in middle school to start the planning process (O'Brien & Mount, 2015). An informal PCP meeting (often known as a "Circle of Friends") would be appropriate and it could include family, friends, and school staff (Taylor, 1997). This is not a formal or legal meeting like an IEP, and it should be a fun and festive occasion for everyone involved.

Inclusion Outside of the Classroom in the School

Both her family and Ms. Garff understand that in many ways it is just as important for Della to be included in school activities as in her classroom so that she can develop and sustain friendships with peers with similar interests. In order to facilitate this inclusion Ms. Garff identifies Della's interests and support needs in different settings and activities, investigate existing school clubs to analyze what might be the best match for Della. From this analysis, Ms. Garff select a school club, the cooking club, for including Della (in part due to Della and her family's enjoyment of musical events). From her analysis and in talking with the cooking club advisor, Ms. Garff decides to briefly talk with the club when Della is not present to ask if two members would be willing to be peer buddies with Della. Two peers, Jessica and Erwin, volunteer and they meet with Ms. Garff and the advisor one afternoon to discuss appropriate supports for Della, and address the learning priorities for Della in the cooking club activities (Pence & Dymond, 2015).

Inclusion Outside of the School Setting

In middle school it is common for students to start developing more extensive friendships and social interactions outside of their family (Azmitia, Kamprath, & Linnet, 1997). This is important for Della as well. It will be important for Della and her family to consider issues of companionship, help, protection, support, similarities in interests, and intimacy and validation (Azmitia et al., 1997; Chadsey & Han, 2005). The issue of reciprocity in Della's friendships will be a critical component for teaching and support so that Della is not only receiving initiations but that she is able to provide reciprocity so that she is perceived as a valued friend by others (Grenot-Scheyer, Staub, Peck, & Schwartz, 1997). It will also be important to consider issues such as find a strong peer network facilitator and how to maintain the peer network over time (Carter et al., 2013).

Della will also need to be connected with her peers with online social media and texting on her smart phone. She will need support from both her family as well as peers to make sure that she is using social media effectively and safely (Grace & Raghavendra, 2019).

Executive Functioning

Initiating Activities and Interactions: Della has difficulty with initiating social interactions and in displays dependent performance (she is often prompt dependent upon staff or peers). To move Della to independence, technology can help her in this area. Della can use an electronic device with applications (App) for schedules, such as First/Then which is a simple App that can be used with photographs from the program, photographs imported, and auditory steps if needed. A schedule can help Della to become familiar with the routines and discriminative stimuli for the commencement of activities. Other apps, such as Pictello, can also be used that have photographic stories created that show steps to initiate and complete an activity. This App also can use imported photographs and auditory instructions (Sprinkle & Miguel, 2013). To address initiating activities and social interactions, Della would benefit from the use of self-talk as a self-management skill (Winsler, Abar, Feder, Schunn, & Rubio, 2007). This can be taught while in the classroom working on assignments as push in from her speech therapist or behavioral support.

Shifting Attention: Della has difficulty with transitions from task to task in the classroom and from location to location in the school outside of the classroom. The use of visual schedules will be helpful for helping Della to transition from task to task as well as from setting to setting. Low tech options are also available for transitions from material to material within task such as the use of a white board in class for providing visual schedules and visual information on task changes.

Use of Technology

With communication is one of Della's biggest challenges, Ms. Garff focuses her technology use on increasing Della's positive social interactions with others. Since Della is often unable to meet her daily communication needs with speech alone, Ms. Garff includes speech-generating devices (SGDs) and mobile technologies with AAC-specific applications for Della. The use of a multistep requesting skills using an iPad loaded with Proloquo2Go proves to be an intervention that increases Della's positive interactions with others (Alzrayer, Banda, & Koul, 2017).

Physical, Medical, Psychological, or Mental Health Issues

Della has a variety of physical and medical needs that need to be addressed in her educational programming. Since it is evident when Della is having a seizure and this could be frightening to peers or cause Della to be stigmatized by peers, Ms. Garff consults with Della's family about the situation. Della's parents tell Ms. Garff that information has been provided to peers in the past. Della's parents recommend a registered nurse, Ms. Zuest, who has previously provided information to Della's peers. Della's family also requests that Della be present when information is presented which Ms. Garff agrees is a good idea. Ms. Garff decides to utilize the bi-weekly School-Wide Positive Behavior Support assembly where rewards and achievements are celebrated at the start of the school day. Ms. Zuest attends one of these assemblies where she does a very brief three-minute presentation on epilepsy and seizures. Later that day she visits each of Della's classes where she and Della do another brief presentation on the specifics of Della's seizures and provide an opportunity to answer any questions that peers or teachers have.

Collaboration

It will be important for Ms. Garff and behavior specialist to collaborate with the school administration and passing periods and lunch supervisors regarding Della's challenging behaviors. It will also be important to provide Della's parents with information on a regular basis (daily through email or some other documented form of communication) regarding Della's challenging behavior and well as her positive behavior in class and around the school so that they can provide reinforcement at home for positive behaviors on Della's part.

Legal Issues

The school needs to ensure that there is adequate supervision of Della during passing periods and lunch times so that appropriate generic antecedent and consequence strategies are implemented (e.g., what would happen when any student is aggressive during those times) as well as the specific protocols in Della's behavior support plan. Any acts of aggression need to be documented according to school policy. The teacher or behavior specialist should provide school supervisors/security staff (who cover passing periods and lunch) as well as any staff who cover for Ms. Slenker when she is on her breaks with written guidelines regarding Della's challenging behaviors.

Discussion Questions

1. Are some students too severely disabled to be included in general education classes, especially from an academic standpoint?
2. Are some students better off in the long run learning functional employment and community skills rather than academic skills?
3. What if Della's peers do not want to interact or be with her in her class or in school activities or in activities outside of the school?
4. Are there some students too severely disabled to be able to partially participate?

References Cited in This Case Study

Agran, M., & Martin, J. (2014). Self-determination: Enhancing competence and independence. In K. Storey & D. Hunter (Eds.), *The road ahead: Transition to adult life for persons with disabilities* (3rd ed., pp. 31–57). Washington, DC: IOS Press.

Alzrayer, N. M., Banda, D. R., & Koul, R. (2017). Teaching children with autism spectrum disorder and other developmental disabilities to perform multistep requesting using an iPad. *AAC: Augmentative and Alternative Communication, 33,* 65-76.

Azmitia, M., Kamprath, N. A., & Linnet, J. (1997). Intimacy and conflict: The dynamics of boys' and girls' friendships during middle childhood and early adolescence. In L. H. Meyer, H. S. Park, M. Grenot-Scheyer, I. S. Schwartz, & B. Harry (Eds.), *Making friends: The Influences of culture and development* (pp. 171–187). Baltimore, MD: Paul H. Brookes Publishing Company.

Ayres, K. M., Lowrey, A., Douglas, K. H., & Sievers, C. (2011). I can identify Saturn but I can't brush my teeth: What happens when the curricular focus for students with severe disabilities shifts. *Education and Training in Autism and Developmental Disabilities, 46,* 11–21.

Baumgart, D., Brown, L., Pumpian, I., Nisbet, J., Ford, A., Sweet, M., Messina, R., & Schroeder, J. (1982). Principle of partial participation and individualized adaptations in educational programs for severely handicapped students. *Journal of the Association for the Severely Handicapped, 7,* 17–27.

Bellamy, G. T., Horner, R. H., & Inman, D. P. (1979). *Vocational habilitation of severely retarded adults: A direct service technology.* Baltimore, MD: University Park Press.

Bernabe, E. A., & Block, M. E. (1994). Modifying rules of a regular girls softball league to facilitate the inclusion of a child with severe disabilities. *Journal of the Association for Persons with Severe Handicaps, 19,* 24–31.

Brown, L., Nietupski, J., & Hamre-Nietupski, S. (1976). Criterion of ultimate functioning. In M. Thomas (Ed.), *Hey, don't forget about me!* (pp. 2–15). Reston, VA: Council for Exceptional Children.

Brown, L., Schwarz, P., Udvari-Solner, A., Kampschroer, E. F., Johnson, F., Jorgensen, J., & Gruenewald, L. (1991). How much time should students with severe intellectual disabilities spend in regular education classrooms and elsewhere? *Journal of the Association for Persons with Severe Handicaps, 16,* 39–47.

Carter, E. W., Asmus, J., Moss, C. K., Cooney, M., Weir, K., Vincent, L., Born, T., Hochman, J. M., Bottema-Beutel, K., & Fesperman, E. (2013). Peer network strategies to foster social connections among adolescents with and without severe disabilities. *Teaching Exceptional Children, 46,* 51–59.

Carter, E. W., Swedeen, B., Walter, M. J., Moss, C. K., & Hsin, C. (2011). Perspectives of young adults with disabilities on leadership. *Career Development for Exceptional Individuals, 34,* 57–67.

Chadsey, J., & Han, K. G. (2005). Friendship-facilitation strategies: What do students in middle school tell us? *Teaching Exceptional Children, 38,* 52–57.

Collins, B. C., Lo, Y., Park, G., & Haughney, K. (2018). Response prompting as an ABA-based instructional approach for teaching students with disabilities. *Teaching Exceptional Children, 50,* 343–355.

Copeland, S. R., McCall, J., Williams, C. R., Guth, C., Carter, E. W., Fowler, S. E., Presley, J. A., & Hughes, C. (2002). High school peer buddies: A win-win situation. *Teaching Exceptional Children, 35,* 16–21

Courtade, G., Spooner, F., Browder, D., & Jimenez, B. (2012). Seven reasons to promote standards-based instruction for students with severe disabilities: A reply to Ayres, Lowrey, Douglas, & Stievers (2011). *Education and Training in Autism and Developmental Disabilities, 47,* 3–13.

Cuvo, A. J. (1978). Validating task analyses of community living skills. *Vocational Evaluation and Work Adjustment Bulletin, 11,* 13–21.

Doyle, M. B., & Giangreco, M. (2013). Guiding principles for including high school students with intellectual disabilities in general education classes. *American Secondary Education, 42,* 57–72.

Ferguson, D. L., & Baumgart, D. (1991). Partial participation revisited. *Journal of the Association for Persons with Severe Handicaps, 16,* 218–227.

Grace, E., & Raghavendra, P. (2019). Cross-age peer e-mentoring to support social media use: A new focus for intervention research. *Communication Disorders Quarterly, 40,* 167–175.

Grenot-Scheyer, M., Staub, D., Peck, C.A., & Schwartz, I. S. (1997). Reciprocity and friendships: Listening to the voice of children and youth with and without disabilities. In L. H. Meyer, H. S. Park, M. Grenot-Scheyer, I. S. Schwartz, & B. Harry, (Eds.), *Making friends: The Influences of culture and development* (pp. 149–167). Baltimore, MD: Paul H. Brookes Publishing Company.

Kreibich, S. R., Chen, M., Reichle, J. (2015). Teaching a child with autism to request breaks while concurrently increasing task engagement. *Language, Speech and Hearing Services in Schools, 46,* 256–265.

Lindsay, S., & Edwards, A. (2013). A systematic review of disability awareness interventions for children and youth. *Disability and Rehabilitation, 35,* 623–646.

Miner, C. A., & Bates, P. E. (1997). The effects of person centered planning activities on the IEP/transition planning process. *Education and Training in Mental Retardation and Developmental Disabilities, 32,* 105–112.

O'Brien, J., & Mount, B. (2015). *Pathfinders: People with developmental disabilities & their allies building communities that work better for everybody.* Toronto, ON, Canada: Inclusion Press.

O'Neill, R. E., Albin, R. H., Storey, K., Horner, R. H., & Sprague, J. R. (2015). *Functional assessment and program development for problem behavior: A practical handbook* (3rd ed.). Stamford, CT: Cengage.

Owen-DeSchryver, J., Carr, E. G., Cale, S., & Blakeley-Smith, A. (2008). Promoting social interactions between students with autism spectrum disorders and their peers in inclusive school settings. *Focus on Autism and Other Developmental Disabilities, 23,* 15–28.

Pence, A. R., & Dymond, S. K. (2015). Extracurricular school clubs: A time for fun and learning. *Teaching Exceptional Children, 47,* 281–288.

Sprinkle, E. C., & Miguel, C. F. (2013). Establishing derived textual activity schedules in children with autism. *Behavioral Interventions, 28*(3), 185–202.

Storey, K. (2002). Strategies for increasing interactions in supported employment settings: An updated review. *Journal of Vocational Rehabilitation, 17,* 231–237.

Storey, K., & Miner, C. (2017). *Systematic instruction of functional skills for students and adults with disabilities* (2nd ed.). Springfield, IL: Charles C Thomas, Publisher, Ltd.

Taylor, G. (1997). Community building in schools: Developing a circle of friends. *Educational and Child Psychology, 14,* 45-50.

Winsler, A., Abar, B., Feder, M. A., Schunn, C., & Rubio, D. A. (2007). Private speech and executive functioning among high-functioning children with Autistic Spectrum Disorders. *Journal of Autism and Developmental Disorders, 37*(9), 1617-1635.

CASE STUDY FOUR: Grigory

Case Study Covers:

- *Learning Disability*
- *High School*

Grigory is a 15-year-old high school student. He lives with his parents and his younger sister. From his teachers' standpoint there are two Grigory's. One Gregory is engaged, charming, and a group leader. However, the other Grigory is difficult and defiant and wants to be left alone. When pressed in class he will sometimes make rude remarks to teachers when asked to perform academic tasks. He plays on the soccer and baseball teams and is a good athlete. Grigory is popular among his peers, has many friends, and is seen by them as someone who is fun to hang out with. On the weekends he volunteers at a homeless shelter where he helps to serve food and also helps individuals with storage issues with clothing and other items.

Grigory's academic performance is very mixed with his doing well in cooperative learning groups but poor in individual work such as on tests. Because of his academic issues, his teachers formed a Student Study Team regarding Grigory. The lead teacher for this group, Ms. Doerr, collects information regarding his academic performance and in the committee discussion it becomes clear that Grigory's difficult and defiant behaviors occur when he is asked to read out loud or if he is asked to read a passage and then present information about the passage right away during the class period. The School Psychologist, Ms. Wong observes Grigory in each of his academic classes using the Functional Assessment Observation Form (O'Neill et al., 2015) and she also interviews Grigory using the Student-Directed Functional Assessment Interview Form (O'Neill et al., 2015). Since Ms. Wong is aware from her review of Grigory's records that he does well in some classes but not in others, she is careful to conduct direct observational assessments when undesirable behaviors are least likely to occur as well as when they are most likely to occur This information concerning when the undesirable behaviors are least likely to occur can often provide valuable information regarding environmental events or establishing operations that are keeping the undesirable behaviors from occurring.

The Student Study Team recommends that Grigory be assessed by a reading disability expert, Ms. Mulkey, who conducts an assessment using the Peabody Individual Achievement Test-Revised (Markwardt, 1989), the Comprehensive Test of Phonological Processing (Wagner, Torgesen, Rashotte, & Pearson, 2013), and the Kaufman Test of Educational Achievement (Kaufman & Kaufman, 2004). These assessments indicate that Grigory's overall reading ability is at the fourth grade level. He has good word recognition for two syllable words but or three or more syllable word recognition causes trouble and in addition, his decoding skills are poor. Grigory has difficulty reading passages and often struggles to understand literal or inferential comprehension questions about the passage. His written expression and spelling were at a fifth grade level. His word recognition fluency and decoding fluency were at a third grade level (his receptive skills precede expressive skills). Grigory has difficulty decoding words (especially multi-syllable words), which deceased his fluency in terms of reading speed, accuracy of decoding, and proper inflection. However, Grigory's listening comprehension, oral expression, and phonological awareness were all very good and are at or close to his grade level.

Accommodations

It would be possible to use an accommodation where Grigory could use different ways to display his knowledge on a subject that does not involve reading out loud or processing written information quickly. For instance, a student could read a passage in a test and then students could divide up into pairs or small groups to discuss the passage. The teacher could provide a scaffolding strategy such as "Pause, Ask Questions, Pause, Review" which would give Grigory (and other students as well) structure for processing information and reaching conclusions.

Modifications

While it could be possible to change the completion level of tasks for Grigory, however, with other supports and interventions it is likely that he will not need any modifications in order to be successful.

Instructional Strategies

Grigory's undesirable behaviors (defiance and rudeness towards teachers) are tied to his academic difficulties related to reading so it will be important to focus on increasing his reading skills as much as possible. These positive academic skills are replacement behaviors for his use of undesirable behaviors to escape from academic reading tasks. Since reading is his most difficult academic task it clearly makes sense to focus interventions on instruction that improves his reading skills (Algozzine, Putnam, & Horner, 2012; Chard, Harn, Sugai, Horner, Simmons, & Kame'enui, 2008; Lin, Morgan, Hillemeier, Cook, Maczuga, & Farkas, 2013).

In order to allow for ongoing assessment of Grigory's skills and to provide information regarding the effectiveness of the intervention procedures, it would be beneficial to use Curriculum-Based Measurement procedures. Since the focus is on ongoing monitoring of student progress, Curriculum-Based Measurement procedures make it efficient and effective for making instructional decisions based upon these formative assessments (Overton, 2015). These assessments occur during the instructional sessions and thus allow the instructor to modify the instruction as needed in a timely manner. For example, it would likely be beneficial for his teacher to have him read aloud from a basal reader for one minute and record the number of words read correctly per minute which would then constitute the decision-making metric for comparison of his future skills in this area to see if the intervention is working or not (Shinn, Knutson, & Nolet, 1990). It will be beneficial for his teacher to assess and monitor his improvement (or lack of) in Grigory's decoding, fluency, and comprehension reading skills. The use of incidental instruction such as cooperative learning, question answering, mapping, scaffolding, and question generation may be effective for increasing Grigory's reading skills. However, these strategies may not be successful for him and more explicit structured instruction may be necessary.

These structured strategies could be "themed instruction" before reading time such as a review of potentially difficult vocabulary words (Williams, 1998), during reading (such as the teacher directing attention to difficult components of the text), and after reading strategies such as asking Grigory to summarize the passage (Lerner & Johns, 2015) and/or activating his background knowledge regarding the content (Ogle, 1986).

It will be important to increase Grigory's reading fluency (the ability to read connected text rapidly, effortlessly, and automatically) by building Grigory's sight vocabulary, his automaticity (knowing how to perform a task at a competent level without requiring conscious effort), and recognizing syllables (Compton, Appleton, & Hosp, 2004; Jennings, Caldwell, & Lerner, 2014). The use of repeated reading, read-along, paired reading, echo reading, and reading aloud to other audiences are interventions that are likely to be beneficial for Grigory (Lerner & Johns, 2015; Nelson, Alber, & Gordy, 2004; Olson, 2014).

In addition to the above skills, reading comprehension will also need to be taught before reading (such as use of text features, observing how text is organized), during reading (use of context clues, identifying the main ideas as he reads), and following the reading (summarizing important points, drawing inferences) (Berkeley & Barber, 2014). Edmonds et al. (2009) recommend that teaching reading comprehension skills should involve modeling, guided practice, independent practice, and corrective feedback.

Another possible intervention for Grigory would be the use of a high-probability sequence for affecting reading fluency within academic assignments and has been shown to increase response rate and establish momentum-like effects on reading behaviors. This intervention alters text difficulty by dividing longer paragraphs into shorter paragraphs, breaking long complex sentences into shorter simple sentences, and replacing multisyllabic terms with simpler synonyms (Vostal & Lee, 2011). The high-probability sequence in reading has been based on increasing response rate and also in increasing reinforcer delivery.

Scaffolded instruction has been an effective support method for many students, including those with a disability. One scaffolding method is the SRA FLEX Literacy approach which uses a gradual-release model involving explicit modeling, guided practice, independent practice, assessment, and maintenance (Martella & Marchand-Martella, 2015).

Related to this strategy would be the use of semantic organizers (such as word webs or hierarchical maps) for reinforcing Grigory's vocabulary development (Berkeley & Barber, 2014).

Another likely beneficial strategy for supporting Grigory would be a four part intervention which used a combination of (a) 20 minutes of skill-level reading mastery, (b) 20 minutes of vocabulary instruction and review/preview of the next day's reading lesson, (c) 10 minutes to define the instructions for the next day's independent practice task, and (d) 10 minutes to teach and review appropriate social skills (e.g., how to request assistance from a teacher and/or peer, and how to ask for a break from a task). This intervention combined effective literacy, instructional intervention, and positive behavior support to build a comprehensive teaching plan (Preciado, Horner, & Baker, 2009).

Supports for Teacher

Since changes in instructional procedures will be necessary for Grigory it will be important that his teachers have "buy in" regarding the plans and also have the "know how" for implementing the interventions. In-service training from or one to one mentoring of the teachers from Ms. Doerr may be necessary for securing the support of others and also ensuring that they have the necessary skills to do so.

Support for Peers

Support for peers is not needed at this point in time as Grigory is well liked by them and he does not engage in any challenging behavior towards them.

Support for Family

Grigory's parents are concerned about his behavior as well as his academic performance. It will be important that Grigory's parents receive information regarding academic and behavioral support strategies. This information should be written in a non-technical language and ideally should provide specific strategies targeted for Grigory with examples of how they can assist him with improving his reading skills.

Positive Behavior Supports

The School Psychologist, Ms. Lee conducted observations of Grigory in his classes and talked with the teachers and it was clear from these sources of information that the function of Grigory's undesirable behaviors is escape from reading tasks. This is a reasonable hypothesis and there is much empirical evidence in the literature that academic difficulties (and often specifically in the area of reading) is often a clear antecedent for undesirable behaviors (Carter & Horner, 2009; Chard et al., 2008; Filter & Horner, 2009; McIntosh, Chard, Boland, & Horner, 2006). For example, McIntosh, Horner, Chard, Dickey, and Braun (2008) found that students with undesirable behaviors whose identified function was to escape academic tasks had lower levels and growth rates in reading skills than students with other identified functions. In addition, they found that these lower skill levels were durable across multiple years and became more discrepant over time.

It could be beneficial to consult with Grigory about a reinforcement system for improving his reading skills and/or reading out loud in class. A reinforcement system for Grigory could be tied into reading at home, progress in sight word vocabulary, and/or an increase in reading fluency.

Social Supports

Grigory has a large number of friends and strong relationships and social networks that meet his support needs so this is not an area of concern for him.

Social Skills Instruction

Grigory may need social skills instruction on how to be more respectful towards teachers in difficult situations as well as increasing his ability to recognize a difficult reading situation and to implement a blocking strategy (such as grasping his hands and engaging in muscle tense and relaxation) so that he does not "blow" and become rude to teachers.

If Grigory does engage in challenging behaviors when he is in a difficult reading situation and he engages in challenging behaviors it would be important for Grigory to learn specific apology skills. A combination of role playing, feedback, modeling, self-recording, self-evaluation, and self-reinforcement would involve a combination of strategies that would make a comprehensive intervention that would be likely to succeed. It will be important that social skills instruction consider the contextual variables of the environment

An important component of this intervention would be in the training in relaxation to the specific use of guided visual imagery to promote relaxation in the situations in which it needed to be used (difficult reading situations). Thus, it was important that Grigory learns to pair the troublesome stimuli with the experience of relaxation to achieve the desired desensitization (Schneider, 1991).

Self-Management Strategies

The team decided (in consultation with Grigory) that Grigory would record the number of times that he handles a difficult academic situation will (self-recording). Grigory decided to graph the number and percentage of well handles situations on a spread sheet so that he received visual feedback (a graph) on how he was doing (self-feedback) and he could then easily share the results with his teachers and others on a daily basis for feedback and encouragement.

Self-Advocacy

In order to be a self-advocate, Grigory needs information on his specific learning disability and how it influences his behavior. That just knowing about self-advocacy with not be enough. The use of the strategies developed by Kim (2003) would be an effective intervention strategy for Grigory. These strategies involved lessons on (1) the concept of assertiveness, (2) non-verbal, paralinguistic, and verbal aspects of assertive behavior, (3) assertive behaviors of requests, refusals, compliments, and understanding interpersonal embarrassment, (4) problem solving, challenging irrational beliefs, and self-management strategies. The instructional strategies suggested by Kim (2003) which were didactic instruction, discussion, modeling, role-playing, feedback, and positive reinforcement.

Self-Determination

Part of being self-determined to is to understand options that are available to is would probably be helpful to briefly describe possible interventions to Grigory so that he can make an informed choice about preferences that he may have for interventions (Agran & Wehmeyer, 2010; Agran, Wehmeyer, Palmer, & Cavin, 2008). The implementation of interventions could be by the general education teacher and with possible additional tutoring or specific instruction from a reading specialist.

Person-Centered Planning

Grigory is approaching his transition from high school to college and/or career. This could be an opportune time to have an informal Person Centered Planning meeting (O'Brien & Mount, 2006; 2015). An informal PCP meeting could include Grigory, his family, friends, and school staff (Falvey, Forest, Pearpoint, & Rosenberg, 1997; Taylor, 1997). It could be combined with PCP meetings involving his friends who could also benefit from planning the transition to adult life.

Inclusion Outside of the Classroom in the School

This is not an area of concern for Grigory.

Inclusion Outside of the School Setting

Grigory is well connected and included outside of the school and thus is not an area of concern.

Executive Functioning

In the area of self-monitoring (meta-cognition), Grigory needs to increase his self-awareness as to when he is confronted with academic work that is difficult. He needs to develop problem solving soling skills in this area. As Grigory progresses academically he will undoubtedly encounter reading and other academic work that is difficult for him and he will need to know how to handle the situation such as a blocking skills like taking a deep breath and counting to five before doing anything. He also needs to be aware of what resources are available for those situations so that he can avoid them if possible (such as learning appropriate academic skills ahead of time or know how to ask for a break so that he can calm down. A way to preload skills is to prepare Grigory for generalized problem-solving skills for reading such as access to texts and reading passages ahead of time. For example, given a text that may have unknown words and/or difficult reading passages, Grigory can choose to have the text read to him from the computer and using the computers accessibility features such as a built in dictionary for definition of words.

Use of Technology

A variety of technology strategies may be helpful for Grigory. The use of videomodeling where Grigory takes videos of his reading passages out loud in order to self-evaluate his strengths as well as his weaknesses could provide helpful feedback these videos could also be spared with his teachers for their input (Laverick, 2014). The use of a variety of electronic methods such as PowerPoint, podcasts, or apps using Grigory's computer, smart phone, and/or other electronic devices in order to review and understand vocabulary words could be helpful. There are a variety of apps and software programs available such as Lexia: Strategies for Older Students (Lexia SOS) or Strategic Reader that Grigory might find useful (Hall, Cohen, Vue, & Ganley, 2015; Kennedy & Deschler, 2010; Kennedy, Thomas, Meyer, Alves, & Lloyd, 2014; Regan, Berkeley, Hughes, & Kirby, 2014).

Grigory is technologically savvy so he may want to try different technology supports for reading such as the use of visual tools like automatic scaffolding and layer concept maps (Yang, 2015), the use of wikis (Lenz, 2014), or a web-based reading annotation system with an attention-based self-regulated learning mechanism (ASRLM) (Chen & Huang, 2014). One or a combination of these strategies might be motivating and reinforcing for him.

Physical, Medical, Psychological, or Mental Health Issues

Grigory does not have any issues or concerns in these areas.

Collaboration

It will be important for Gregory's teachers to collaborate with each other and share their ideas with Grigory and his parents. This communication with he and his parents could include a blog post. emails, texts, teacher/parent/student meetings, and/or regular progress reports (Storey & Post, 2017).

Legal Issues

It may be beneficial for Grigory to receive 504 accommodations or that he receive services under the Individuals with Disabilities Education Act (Giuliani, 2012; Siegel, 2017). It is Grigory's legal right to these services if he qualifies for them so he and his family as well as the educational staff should not hesitate to advocate for appropriate services if he will benefit from them (Colker & Waterstone, 2011). A recommendation from the Student Study Team may be the to start for receiving these services.

Discussion Questions

1. Is academic instruction by itself enough to reduce Grigory's undesirable behaviors or are positive behavior supports needed as well?
2. Since Grigory appears to be doing well with his many meaningful activities outside of school, how important is it to increase his reading level since he seems to be doing well in life with his current reading abilities?
3. Would Grigory benefit more from being in Resource Room rather than receiving services in the general education classroom?

References Cited in This Case Study

Agran, M., Wehmeyer, M., Palmer, S., & Cavin, M. (2008). Promoting student active classroom participation skills through instruction to promote self-regulated learning and self-determination. *Career Development for Exceptional Individuals, 31,* 106–114.

Agran, M., & Wehmeyer, M. (2010). Promoting self-regulated learning. In A. Mourad & J. de la Fuente Arias (Eds.), *International perspectives on applying self-regulated learning in different settings* (pp. 205–224). New York: Peter Lang Publishing.

Algozzine, R., Putnam, R., & Horner, R. (2012). Support for teaching students with learning disabilities academic skills and social behaviors within a response-to-intervention model: Why it doesn't matter what comes first. *Insights on Learning Disabilities: From Prevailing Theories to Validated Practices, 9*(1), 7–36.

Berkeley, S., & Barber, A. T. (2014). *Maximizing effectiveness of reading comprehension instruction in diverse classrooms.* Baltimore: Paul H. Brookes Publishing Co.

Carter, D. R., & Horner, R. H. (2009). Adding functional behavioral assessment to First Step to Success: A case study. *Journal of Positive Behavior Interventions, 11,* 22–34.

Chard, D., Harn, B., Sugai, G., Horner, R., Simmons, D. C., & Kame'enui, E. (2008). Core features of multi-tiered systems of reading and behavioral support. In C. Greenwood, T. Kratochwill, & M. Clements (Eds.), *Schoolwide prevention models: lessons learned in elementary schools* (pp. 31–60). New York, NY: Guilford Press.

Chen, C. M., & Huang, S. H. (2014). Web-based reading annotation system with an attention-based self-regulated learning mechanism for promoting reading performance. *British Journal of Educational Technology, 45,* 959–980.

Colker, R., & Waterstone, J. K. (2011). *Special education advocacy.* New Providence, NJ: LexisNexis.

Compton, D. L., Appleton, A. C., & Hosp, M. K. (2004). Exploring the relationship between text-leveling systems and reading accuracy and fluency in second-grade students who are average and poor decoders. *Learning Disabilities Research & Practice, 19,* 176–184.

Edmonds, M. S., Vaughn, S., Wexler, J., Reutebuch, C., Cable, A., Tackett, K. K., & Schnakenberg, J. W. (2009). A synthesis of reading interventions and effects on reading comprehension outcomes for older struggling students. *Review of Educational Research, 79,* 262–300.

Falvey, M., Forest, M., Pearpoint, J., & Rosenberg, R. (1997). *All my life's a circle: Using the Tools: Circles, MAPS and PATH.* Toronto, ON, Canada: Inclusion Press.

Filter, K. J., & Horner, R. H. (2009). Function-based academic interventions for problem behavior. *Education and Treatment of Children, 32,* 1–20.

Giuliani, G. A. (2012). *The comprehensive guide to special education law: Over 400 frequently asked questions and answers every educator needs to know about the legal rights of exceptional children and their parents.* Philadelphia, PA: Jessica Kingsley Publishers.

Hall, T. E., Cohen, N., Vue, G., & Ganley, P. (2015). Addressing Learning Disabilities with UDL and technology: Strategic Reader. *Learning Disability Quarterly, 38,* 72–83.

Jennings, J. H., Caldwell, J. S., & Lerner, J. W. (2014). *Reading problems: Assessment and teaching strategies* (7th ed.). Boston, MA: Pearson.

Kaufman, A. S., & Kaufman, N. L. (2004). *Kaufman test of educational achievement* (2nd ed.). Circle Pine, MN: AGS Publishing.

Kennedy, M. J., & Deschler, D. D. (2010). Literacy instruction, technology, and students with learning disabilities: Research we have, research we need. *Learning Disability Quarterly, 33,* 289–298.

Kennedy, M. J., Thomas, C. N., Meyer, J. P., Alves, K. D., & Lloyd, J. W. (2014). Using evidence-based multimedia to improve vocabulary performance of adolescents with LD: A UDL approach. *Learning Disability Quarterly, 37,* 71–86.

Kim, Y. (2003). The effects of assertiveness training on enhancing the social skills of adolescents with visual impairments. *Journal of Visual Impairment and Blindness, 97,* 285–297.

Laverick, D. M. (2014). Supporting striving readers through technology-based instruction. *Reading Improvement, 51,* 11–19.

Lenz, C. (2014). Can we talk? A model for active reading comprehension using technology. *Journal of Adolescent and Adult Literacy, 58,* 109–109.

Lerner, J. W., & Johns, B. H. (2015). *Learning disabilities and related disabilities: Strategies for success* (13th ed.). Stamford, CT: Cengage.

Lin, Y., Morgan, P. L., Hillemeier, M., Cook, M., Maczuga, S., & Farkas, G. (2013). Reading, mathematics, and behavioral difficulties interrelate: Evidence from a cross-lagged panel design and population-based sample of US upper elementary students. *Behavioral Disorders, 38,* 212–227.

Martella, R. C., & Marchand-Martella, N. E. (2015). Improving classroom behavior through effective instruction: An illustrative program example using SRA FLEX Literacy. *Education and Treatment of Children, 38,* 241–271.

Markwardt, F. C. (1989). *Peabody individual achievement test-revised.* Circle Pine, MN: AGS Publishing.

McIntosh, K., Chard, D., Boland, J., & Horner, R. H. (2006). Demonstration of combined efforts in school-wide academic and behavioral systems and incidence of reading and behavior challenges in early elementary grades. *Journal of Positive Behavior Interventions, 8,* 146–154.

McIntosh, K., Horner, R. H., Chard, D. J., Dickey, C. R., & Braun, D. H. (2008). Reading skills and function of problem behavior in typical school settings. *Journal of Special Education, 41,* 131–147.

Nelson, J., Alber, S., & Gordy, A. (2004). Effects of systematic error correction and repeated readings on the reading accuracy and proficiency of second graders with disabilities. *Education and Treatment of Children, 27,* 186–198.

O'Brien, J., & Mount, B. (2006). *Make a difference: A guidebook for person-centered direct support.* Toronto, ON, Canada: Inclusion Press.

O'Brien, J., & Mount, B. (2015). *Pathfinders: People with developmental disabilities & their allies building communities that work better for everybody.* Toronto, ON, Canada: Inclusion Press.

Ogle, D. M. (1986). K-W-L: A teaching model that develops active reading of expository text. *Reading Teacher, 39,* 564–570.

Olson, P. (2014). Weaker readers as experts: Preferential instruction and the fluency improvement of lower performing student tutors. *Reading Improvement, 51,* 32–40.

O'Neill, R. E., Albin, R. W., Storey, K., Horner, R. H., & Sprague, J. R. (2015). *Functional assessment and program development for problem behavior: A practical handbook* (3rd ed.). Stamford, CT: Cengage Publishing Company.

Overton, T. (2015). *Assessing learners with special needs: An applied approach* (8th ed.). Boston, MA: Pearson.

Preciado, J., Horner, R. H., & Baker, S. (2009). Using a function-based approach to decrease problem behavior and increase academic engagement for Latino English Language Learners. *Journal of Special Education, 42,* 227–240.

Regan, K., Berkeley, S., Hughes, M., & Kirby, S. (2014). Effects of computer-assisted instruction for struggling elementary readers with disabilities. *Journal of Special Education, 48,* 106–119.

Schneider, B. H. (1991). A comparison of skill-building and desensitization strategies for intervention with aggressive children. *Aggressive Behavior, 17,* 301–311.

Shinn, M. R., Knutson, N., & Nolet, V. (1990). Best practices in curriculum-based measurement. In A. Thomas & J. Grimes (Eds.), *Best practices in school psychology* (2nd ed., pp. 287–308). Washington, DC: National Association of School Psychologists.

Siegel, L. M. (2017). *The complete IEP guide: How to advocate for your special ed child* (9th ed.). Berkeley, CA: Nolo.

Storey, K., & Post, M. (2017). *Positive behavior supports in classrooms and schools: Effective and practical strategies for teachers and other service providers* (2nd ed.). Springfield, IL: Charles C Thomas, Publisher, Ltd.

Taylor, G. (1997). Community building in schools: Developing a circle of friends. *Educational and Child Psychology, 14,* 45–50.

Vostal, B. R., & Lee, D. L. (2011). Behavioral momentum during a continuous reading task: An exploratory study. *Journal of Behavioral Education, 20,* 163–181.

Wagner, R., Torgesen, J., Rashotte, C., & Pearson, N. (2013). *Comprehensive test of phonological processing* (2nd ed.). Pro-Ed. Austin, TX.

Williams, J. P. (1998). Improving the comprehension of disabled readers. *Annals of Dyslexia, 48,* 213–238.

Yang, Y. F. (2015). Automatic scaffolding and measurement of concept mapping for EFL students to write summaries. *Journal of Educational Technology and Society, 18,* 273–286.

CASE STUDY FIVE: Rhia

Case Study Covers:

- *Intellectual Disabilities*
- *High School*

Rhia is a seventeen-year-old high school junior who enjoys soccer (playing and watching), riding horses, hanging out with her friends, and going camping with her family and through her scouting group. Rhia plays on a soccer team through the city parks and recreation department and her family takes her to a barn for horseback riding lessons (her older sister Gertrude also used to take lessons there). Generally speaking, Rhia is upbeat and outgoing with her family and friends in school though she does have a stubborn streak and can become non-compliant and refuse to do things. Rhia also has Down Syndrome and an intellectual disability. A lot of people who know her attribute her stubbornness to her having Down Syndrome.

Academically Rhia does okay in school, passes all her classes, and is on track for graduation. Rhia does receive support from a Resource Teacher, Ms. Roberts, and an inclusion specialist, Mr. Blandy. Rhia is fully included into general education classes (as she has been throughout her schooling) and does well in academic tasks that are concrete such as spelling, math, and science. She does less well in academic subjects that are more abstract such as history and literature. Mr. Blandy provides "push in" supports for students and he usually overlaps with Rhia in one class period per week (rotating through her different classes). Rhia also receives academic support from Ms. Roberts where she is generally pulled out one period a day (during the physical education class so that she is not missing academic content instruction and she receives her physical education credits through soccer and horseback riding) to get help with homework assignments and additional academic instruction on topics being covered in classes.

Rhia does struggle a bit with executive functioning skills. In the area of executive functioning skills, Rhia is strong in initiating activities such as getting together with friends and her soccer and horseback riding activities. Rhia struggles with executive functioning areas of emotional control and inhibiting impulses and in organizational skills such as keeping track of homework and class assignments.

Rhia and her family want her to have a real job in the community when she graduates from high school and starts receiving supports from the adult service system. Rhia is not interesting in attending college at this time but says that she may consider it when she is older and has shown that she can be successful at work.

Accommodations

Rhia is below grade level on her skills for reading from print but she can access information better with "read aloud" text so as an accommodations she uses audio books with the same textbook every other student is reading may be an accommodation for students with print disabilities in the area of reading comprehension.

Modifications

Mr. Blandy, Ms. Roberts, and Rhia's teachers understand that Rhia will benefit from having some of her academic curriculum modified. Together, they decide upon a variety of strategies:

Input: This adapts the way instruction is delivered to Rhia. In classes with more abstract concepts (such as history and literature) increasing the number of concrete examples helps Rhia (as well as other students) to understand the information

Output: This adapts how Rhia can show that she understands the information in classes. For oral and group presentations, Rhia focuses on concrete topics such as timelines in history class and biographical information on authors in literature.

Instructional Strategies

A variety of universal design instructional strategies help Rhia, as well as other students in her classes, with academic learning. These strategies include cooperative learning, question answering, mapping, scaffolding, question generation, themed instruction, review of vocabulary, and teacher direction to difficult dimensions of the text. In her pull out sessions with Rhia, Ms. Roberts uses semantic organizers (such as word webs or hierarchical maps) for reinforcing vocabulary development (Berkeley & Barber, 2014) and Ms. Robert's also follows the guidelines developed by Preciado, Horner, and Baker (2009) which uses a combination of (a) 20 minutes of skill-level reading mastery, (b) 20 minutes of vocabulary instruction and review/preview of the next day's reading lesson, (c) 10 minutes to define the instructions for the next day's independent practice task, and (d) 10 minutes to teach and review appropriate social skills (e.g., how to request assistance from a teacher and/or peer, and how to ask for a break from a task).

Supports for Teachers

Ms. Roberts and Mr. Blandy work closely with Rhia's teachers in developing lessons and curriculum that plays to Rhia's strengths. They take the lead in developing materials and instructional methods such as using multiple examples are errorless learning in teaching concepts. Both Ms. Roberts and Mr. Blandy stress to the teachers that these methods are helpful to a variety of students in the class as well as for Rhia. The teachers appreciate the support and collaboration in the development of these lessons, and they see the benefit for all of the students in the classes.

Support for Peers

Rhia has been in elementary and middle school with most of her general education peers and they are familiar with and support of Rhia. Most of them see her as another peer and are more interested in her interests in soccer and horses and less interested in her disability.

Support for Family

Rhia's family have been pleased with her education and inclusion in school throughout the years. They, however, are unsure about what will happen to Rhia once she leaves the K-12 system upon graduation. At back to school nights and at Rhia's IEP meetings they ask Mr.

Blandy and Ms. Roberts for information on the transition to the adult service system. The information that is shared with them is very helpful as there are different legal rights and service delivery models that they must understand in order to support Rhia. Mr. Blandy and Ms. Jackson make sure that Rhia's family is connected with advocacy organizations and parent support groups to help them navigate these new systems.

Positive Behavior Supports

Mr. Blandy understands that Rhia's "stubbornness" is not due to her having Down Syndrome but that her behavior is controlled by Rhia's interaction with her environment. Mr. Blandy first develops an operational definition of Rhia's non-compliance behavior:

> *Non-Compliance:* Not engaging in requested behavior within 10 seconds of a given staff request. *Positive Examples (occurrences) include:* laying on floor, throwing instructional item, putting head down, moving away from instructional area within three seconds of being given an instruction, and saying "no" or other refusal words. *Negative Examples (non-occurrence) include:* Making attempt at work but doing work incorrectly, taking off her shoes, looking at peers or teacher.

Mr. Blandy observes Rhia in different academic classes using the Functional Assessment Observation Form (O'Neill, Albin, Storey, Horner, & Sprague, 2015) and he also interviews her using the Student-Directed Functional Assessment Interview Form (O'Neill et al., 2015). Since Mr. Blandy is aware Rhia does better in some subject areas than in others, he is careful to conduct direct observational assessments when non-compliance behaviors are least likely to occur as well as when they are most likely to occur This information concerning when the non-compliance behaviors are least likely to occur can often provide valuable information regarding environmental events or establishing operations that are keeping the undesirable behaviors from occurring.

From the information collected it becomes clear to Mr. Blandy that Rhia's non-compliance behavior is most likely to occur when she is given an instruction that is not clear to her and when the instruction involves three or more steps (such as get your notebook out, go to your group area, go over the group rules and roles, perform the experiment, and then individually write your notes out). Thus, the function of Rhia's non-compliance was to escape from situations where the directions were not clear to her.

Mr. Blandy confers with Rhia's teachers about the situation and with the teacher's feedback, he decides to teach Rhia to say the phrase "could you please write the instructions on the white board" when she is not clear about what to do. This provides information and clearer directions to Rhia and also to other students in the class who may not be clear on the instructions or need a reminder once the activity is underway.

Social Supports

Since Rhia sometimes has difficulty understanding and writing down homework assignments, Mr. Blandy recruits two volunteers in each class (in case one is absent) to assist Rhia in understanding and writing down homework assignments at the end of each class. These peers also assist Rhia in putting any handouts for each class in the notebook's pocket page.

Social Skills Instruction

Since Rhia sometimes does not take direction well from teachers, Mr. Blandy decides that specific instruction needs to occur for Rhia to learn skills for handling these situations. Other students in classes also have difficulty in this area so Mr. Blandy decides that a group instruction method would be appropriate. Mr. Blandy locates a lesson from the Skillstreaming program on Responding to Difficult Requests. He knew he could appropriately include a role-play for "responding to teacher requests" into the lesson scenarios. The Skillstreaming lesson was included in the social studies period right after lunch break when the students enjoyed active role-plays. After having students provide examples of difficult requests (luckily one example included a teacher asking a student to do an assignment over). Mr. Blandy modeled the steps to use for responding. These steps were: (a) listen to what the other person is requesting, (b) restate back what you understand the person is asking, (c) if you disagree, ask the other person to explain anything you don't agree with, (d) if you still disagree, politely provide the person with the information and reason you feel or think differently, and (e) stop and think about the person's response and the best way to handle the situation. Mr. Blandy guided students through the role-plays and provided immediate corrections if steps were missed and provided praise for correct performance.

Self-Management Strategies

Rhia often struggles with her organizational ability. One area in particular with which Rhia has difficulty is organizing her homework assignments and storing them in her backpack. When in class, Rhia follows directions to write her homework down, which is done on a piece of paper from his loose-leaf binder. Once her homework is written down, Rhia stuffs the homework assignment paper in her backpack, along with any related homework handouts. Once at home and ready to work, Rhia has difficulty finding her homework materials and assignments for each of her academic classes. Se dumps out the contents of her backpack, which usually consist of crumpled up school papers, broken pencils, and various collected gadgets. When the homework papers are found (often in a jumbled ball), they are usually torn, wrinkled, and unreadable. This has caused such frustration and anxiety for both Rhia and her parents.

Rhia's parents and teachers are worried about her lack of organization skills as it is negatively impacting her academic progress in all her classes. A meeting was held with Rhia, two of her teachers, Mr. Blandy, and Rhia's parents to see what could be done to help Rhia. It was decided that Rhia needed a better strategy for how she records her homework and how she stores homework handouts in her backpack (other than the haphazard strategy she's currently using). It was also discussed that due to the fact that Rhia has multiple teachers and moves from class to class, she needs a way to learn to manage this organization independently, yet be able to receive feedback from her teachers and parents that this management system is working and that her homework assignments are completed.

Everyone thought it was a good idea when Mr. Blandy proposed the use of a self-management system for organizing her backpack that she could use at both school and home. For this system, Rhia and her father went shopping and bought four different colored spiral notebooks, one for each academic class. Additionally, each notebook came with a two-sided pocket page.

Rhia's English teacher and Mr. Blandy also design a daily check-off list with the step-by-step instructions for Rhia to follow for homework (this checklist was also made available to all students in the class and many of them used it and found it very helpful). This daily check-off list provided a section for each class. After each class, Rhia would assess whether she followed the steps on the checklist for organizing her homework materials and check off the boxes indicating completion for each completed step. If she missed a step, she would go back and complete it. Once this was done, she would seek out the teacher to confirm she had used the system correctly. The teacher would then confirm by initialing the section filled out for that class. Mr. Blandy showed this system to other teachers and they all agreed to use it with Rhia and make it available for other students in their classes. Everyone agreed that in order to have a well-organized backpack, the following steps would be on the form:

- homework written in notebook,
- handouts and/or materials placed in notebook pocket,
- notebook put in backpack,
- book, if needed, put in backpack
- pens, pencils, and erasers inside backpack pocket,
- other items and gadgets in inside backpack pocket,
- no wrappers and garbage in backpack.

Also included on the form is a line for each teacher and one parent to sign and date confirming that Rhia correctly followed instruction along with any comments for corrective feedback, if needed. This way both teachers and parents would be able to communicate to Rhia and each other about how the system was working.

At home, Rhia's parents agreed that one of them would sign the form when homework had been completed and the checklist steps followed for returning work into the correct notebook pocket and all materials into the backpack. For a further incentive, Rhia's mother helped Rhia tp make a list of special rewards she liked. On Fridays, Rhia and her parents review the week's self-management forms, and if Rhia was successful in most classes (75%) on four out of five days, she would choose a reward from the list.

Self-Determination

Martin and Marshall (1995) have conceptualized that individuals who are self-determined establish goals from an awareness of their needs and interests, then develop plans, implement the plans, self-evaluate progress, and make needed adjustments to attain their goals. It is important that Rhia develop self-determination in her life as individuals who are self-determined have higher employment rates and post-school success than those who are not self-determined (Wehmeyer & Schwartz, 1997). As part of this self-determination Rhia must have meaningful choices to choose from (Agran, Storey, & Krupp, 2010). These meaningful choices may be derived from her self-directed IEP. Bambara, Cole, and Koger (1998) recommend that four components of support need to be put in place to help facilitate self-determination. These are: (a) know the person, (b) build an option rich lifestyle, (c) teach self-determination skills, and (d) create supportive social contexts.

Rhia will need instruction and supports for running her self-directed IEP. Mr. Blandy decides that the Self-Directed IEP curriculum developed by Martin, Marshall, Maxson, and Jerman (1996) would be appropriate for Rhia as this curriculum teaches students how to become actively involved and take a leadership role at their own IEP meeting. It involves a multi-media package consisting of a video depicting a student modeling the 11 steps of the Self-Directed IEP process, a teacher manual with scripted lessons, and a 27-page student workbook.

In addition, Rhia would benefit from learning leadership skills related to self-advocacy. The People First organization provides advocacy training for people with intellectual disabilities and Rhia could benefit from being connected with this organization (http://www.peoplefirst.org). Another method would be to connect Rhia with a mentorship program for youth (Carter, Swedeen, Walter, Moss, & Hsin, 2011). This would not necessarily have to be a program specifically designed for youth with disabilities but could be a generic program such as those offered by school districts, community colleges, or private organizations such as boys/girls clubs, YMCAs, or cultural organizations.

Person-Centered Planning

Person-centered planning will be a key component for developing an appropriate and successful intervention for Rhia. Ms. Roberts supports Rhia in developing a self-directed IEP/ITP to help ensure that her school objectives and outcomes are what she desires (Martin & Williams-Diehm, 2013). Ms. Roberts follows the recommendations by Woods, Sylvester, and Martin (2010) that students be taught content knowledge about the transition process and then develop a script that provides information for the student to lead a discussion regarding their academic and functional performance, interests, post-school and transition goals, and connecting with adult support services.

Inclusion Outside of the Classroom in the School

Mr. Blandy understands that it is important for Rhia to be included in all aspects of school life. Rhia, her family, and Mr. Blandy meet to go over the various clubs at the school and Mr. Blandy briefly describes each club. To the surprise of her family and Mr. Blandy, Rhia decides that she is most interested in the Stagecraft club. Mr. Blandy arranges for Rhia to meet with the advisor and two of the students in the club that Rhia knows. They explain to Rhia and Mr. Blandy that Stagecraft is focused all aspects of producing a play or musical. They all agree that Rhia should first come to a planning meeting and then a Saturday afternoon work time where the club is starting work on the set of the fall play. These two meeting will provide opportunities for Rhia to better understand what is involved in being a member of the club and if she wants to continue with the club or not.

Inclusion Outside of the School Setting

Rhia is well included and connected with her community outside of school through her soccer and horseback riding activities. It is important to note that none of these activities are specifically designated for people with disabilities which may be advantageous for community inclusion.

Executive Functioning

Rhia struggles with executive functioning areas of emotional control and inhibiting impulses and in organizational skills such as keeping track of homework and class assignments.

Emotional Control and Meta Cognition: Rhia sometimes has difficulty managing her emotional responses appropriately. Ms. Roberts and Mr. Blandy decide that the use of an auditory prompting procedure would be an appropriate self-management method for self-evaluation regarding her emotional control in certain situations. They also decide to combine it with a self-reinforcement system. Currently, Rhia does not have the ability to self-evaluate her behaviors and she does not have a formal self-monitoring system in place. The auditory prompting procedures are used for self-monitoring and self-evaluating her behaviors including her inhibiting impulses and emotional control behaviors (Post, Montgomery, & Storey, 2009).

Shifting Attention: Rhia has difficulty with transitions from task to task in the classroom. She finds the use of visual schedules to be helpful for helping her transition from task to task. Ms. Roberts and Rhia find that some low-tech options for transitions from material to material within task such as the use of a white board in class for providing visual schedules and visual information on task changes work best for Rhia. These strategies are ones that will help Rhia and also other students in the classes as well.

Use of Technology

The use of social media is one of Rhia's biggest challenges as this is the way in which her peers tend to communicate with each other. It can be difficult for Rhia to keep current with developments in social media and also in navigating the social nuances in her online interactions. Rhia's family walks a fine line in helping and protecting her and in allowing her independence in her online presence. Her siblings and peers keep Rhia up to date on what to use online and her parents use parental safeguards to keep Rhia safe.

Physical, Medical, Psychological, or Mental Health Issues

Physical and medical components are not of concern for Rhia as she is in good physical and mental health.

Collaboration

There are many players involved with Rhia's between her family at home, her school-based program, and district personnel. This case requires collaboration, consultation skills, and an ability to use non-technical language so that all collaborators are included and have a say in the programming. Mr. Blandy understands this, and he develops a list of roles and responsibilities for each component of Rhia's instructional program.

Legal Issues

There are currently no concerns with legal issues as Rhia is receiving services outlined in her IEP. However, once she graduates from high school, she will be receiving services from agencies in the adult service system and thus her parents will need to be aware of legal issues that may arise in transition to those services.

Discussion Questions

1. Should individuals with intellectual disabilities receive recreational services through those designed specifically for people with disabilities or should they access regular recreational programs?
2. Not all students with intellectual disabilities can keep up with academic demands in general education classes like Rhia can. Should those students who struggle academically be placed in general education classrooms?
3. If Rhia had started out in a special day class specifically designed for students with intellectual disabilities would she have achieved the academic outcome of graduating from high school?

References Cited in This Case Study

Agran, M., & Martin, J. (2014). Self-determination: Enhancing competence and independence. In K. Storey & D. Hunter (Eds.), *The road ahead: Transition to adult life for persons with disabilities* (3rd ed., pp. 31–57). Washington, DC: IOS Press.

Agran, M., Storey, K., & Krupp, M. (2010). Choosing and choice making are not the same: Asking "what do you want for lunch?" is not self-determination. *Journal of Vocational Rehabilitation, 33,* 77–88.

Bambara, L. M., Cole, C. L., & Koger, F. (1998). Translating self-determination concepts into supports for adults with severe disabilities. *Journal of the Association for Persons with Severe Handicaps, 23,* 27–37.

Berkeley, S., & Barber, A. T. (2014). *Maximizing effectiveness of reading comprehension instruction in diverse classrooms.* Baltimore: Paul H. Brookes Publishing Co.

Carter, E. W., Asmus, J., Moss, C. K., Cooney, M., Weir, K., Vincent, L., Born, T., Hochman, J. M., Bottema-Beutel, K., & Fesperman, E. (2013). Peer network strategies to foster social connections among adolescents with and without severe disabilities. *Teaching Exceptional Children, 46,* 51–59.

Carter, E. W., Swedeen, B., Walter, M. J., Moss, C. K., & Hsin, C. (2011). Perspectives of young adults with disabilities on leadership. *Career Development for Exceptional Individuals, 34,* 57–67.

Martin, J. E., & Marshall, L. H. (1995). ChoiceMaker: A comprehensive self-determination transition program. *Intervention in School and Clinic, 30,* 147–156.

Martin, J. E., Marshall, L. H., Maxson, L. M., & Jerman, P. L. (1996). *The self-directed IEP.* Longmont, CO: Sopris West.

Martin, J. E., & Williams-Diehm, K. (2013). Student engagement and leadership of the transition planning process. *Career Development and Transition for Exceptional Individuals, 36,* 43–50.

O'Brien, J., & Mount, B. (2015). *Pathfinders: People with developmental disabilities & their allies building communities that work better for everybody.* Toronto, ON, Canada: Inclusion Press.

O'Neill, R. E., Albin, R. H., Storey, K., Horner, R. H., & Sprague, J.R. (2015). *Functional assessment and program development for problem behavior: A practical handbook* (3rd ed.). Stamford, CT: Cengage.

Post, M., Montgomery, J., & Storey, K. (2009). A decision tree for the use of auditory prompting strategies. *Journal of Vocational Rehabilitation, 31*(1), 51–54.

Preciado, J., Horner, R. H., & Baker, S. (2009). Using a function-based approach to decrease problem behavior and increase academic engagement for Latino English Language Learners. *Journal of Special Education, 42,* 227–240.

Wehmeyer, M. L., & Schwartz, M. (1997). Self-determination and positive adult outcomes: A follow-up study of youth with mental retardation or learning disabilities. *Exceptional Children, 63,* 245–255.

Woods, L. L., Sylvester, L., & Martin, J. E. (2010). Student-directed transiton planning: Increasing student knowledge and self-efficacy in the transition planning process. *Career Development for Exceptional Individuals, 33,* 106–114.

Section Two

**CASE STUDIES WITH
PARTIAL ANALYSIS**

CASE STUDY SIX: Hubert

Case Study Covers:

- *Traumatic Brain Injury*
- *Elementary School*

Hubert is in the second grade. He enjoys school very much. Hubert is outgoing and likes to interact with peers as well as with the adults at the school. He is well liked by pretty much everyone. At school he likes academics, recess, and free play time where he and his friends play with Legos and other building toys. Hubert recently acquired a disability when he was in an accident when he was riding his bike and was hit by a car (fortunately he was wearing a helmet). Unfortunately, he sustained a Traumatic Brain Injury (TBI), which put him in the hospital for several months. Hubert received a closed head injury to the left side of his head. His medical diagnosis suggested that it would be likely that Hubert would have cognitive deficits such as impaired attention, reduced processing speed, distractibility, and deficits in executive functions. Following his hospitalization Hubert returned to his second-grade class a month ago. He does not have an IEP or a 504 Plan. Since returning to school Hubert has gotten behind academically from being in the hospital. Since his injury he becomes easily distracted and has a hard time focusing on his work.

In addition, he has started to become upset and meltdowns when he can't do the work and lash out at others. These meltdowns involve Hubert becoming highly anxious where he starts hyperventilating, sweating, pacing, and mumbling to himself. Hubert will then often start yelling at others, especially his teacher, Ms. Grosche, and blame them for his inability to concentrate and do his work. Hubert feels very remorseful after these episodes which only increases his stress level even more. Hubert lives at home with his parents and older sister and younger brother. Hubert is also displaying the same behaviors at home that he has started engaging in at school and of course his parents are very concerned about him.

Case Study Evaluation Guided Practice

Below are the areas to assess based upon best practices in inclusive education for students with disabilities. Not all of the areas listed may apply to this case study. However, it is important to consider all of them in analyzing academic and support needs and then determining how to successfully build and implement those supports. It is important to have a positive vision of the future for the person, to be comprehensive, and to be creative.

Consider the Following Areas in this Case Study

Accommodations
Modifications
Instructional Strategies
Supports for Teacher
Support for Peers
Support for Family
Positive Behavior Supports
Social Supports
Social Skills Instruction
Self-Management Strategies
Self-Advocacy
Self-Determination
Person-Centered Planning
Inclusion Outside of the Classroom in the School
Inclusion Outside of the School Setting
Executive Functioning
Use of Technology
Physical, Medical, Psychological, or Mental Health Issues
Collaboration
Legal Issues

CASE STUDY SEVEN: Lorelie

Case Study Covers:

- *Deafness and Hearing Impairment*
- *Elementary School*

Lorelie is a fifth-grade student who is deaf. Lorelie was born deaf and has been taught to read lips and to talk using her voice. Her parents and older brother do not have deafness or hearing impairments and her parents want Lorelie to be as "normal" as possible and not to stand out or look different from her peers by using sign language. She has an IEP and she receives speech and language services of one hour per week. Lorelie struggles both academically and socially at school. Academically she receives information visually and not through hearing. Like many students who are deaf, Lorelie can understand about 30 to 45 percent of the words being spoken to her through lip reading (partially because many words look the same even though they sound different, it can be challenging to try and read lips and follow written information simultaneously, and that speakers often do not directly face her when talking or may turn away from her). Lorelie struggles to gather a full message based solely on lip reading, though she is pretty skilled at interpreting facial cues, body language, and context to assist in figuring out information. Part of the problem is that there are often questions and comments from students in classes where she cannot read their lips (for example, if they are sitting behind her as she prefers to sit in the front of class so that she can see the teacher's lips better.

Lorelie also struggles in her academic work. She has a hard time understanding abstract material as well as mathematic calculations. She is getting further and further behind academically which is decreasing her motivation to do her work in class.

Social interactions can also be difficult for Lorelie as she finds it hard to keep track of back and forth interactions in a group of people. She prefers to interact one on one with her peers, but they often prefer to interact in groups.

At home Lorelie enjoys playing basketball, arts and crafts projects, cooking, and quilting (she and her mother work on quilts together). Lorelie has been having fewer and fewer get together with friends which worries her parents as she is often spending time alone at home on the weekends and doesn't want to go out.

Case Study Evaluation Guided Practice

Below are the areas to assess based upon best practices in inclusive education for students with disabilities. Not all the areas listed may apply to this case study. However, it is important to consider all of them in analyzing academic and support needs and then determining how to successfully build and implement those supports. It is important to have a positive vision of the future for the person, to be comprehensive, and to be creative.

Consider the Following Areas in this Case Study

Accommodations
Modifications
Instructional Strategies
Supports for Teacher
Support for Peers
Support for Family
Positive Behavior Supports
Social Supports
Social Skills Instruction
Self-Management Strategies
Self-Advocacy
Self-Determination
Person-Centered Planning
Inclusion outside of the Classroom in the School
Inclusion Outside of the School Setting
Executive Functioning
Use of Technology

Physical, Medical, Psychological, or Mental Health Issues
Collaboration
Legal Issues

CASE STUDY EIGHT: Yumi

Case Study Covers:

- *Visual Impairment*
- *Middle School*

Yumi is a 12-year-old student with a visual impairment (her primary disability) and a mild learning disability of Dyscalculia (her secondary disability). Yumi attends her local middle school where she is "mainstreamed" into some general education classes (art, social studies, and homeroom). She spends the rest of her time in a resource classroom for students with disabilities. Yumi does receive adaptive physical education services. She also receives Mobility and Orientation services (she currently uses a cane when using public transportation or out in the community but does not use it at school and she does not use or have a guide dog) and she is independent in using the local transportation system.

Yumi does okay academically and is generally on grade level though it is starting to be more difficult for her to keep up with assignments and homework and also to understand the academic material as it gets more complex. If handouts or worksheets are used in class, she generally needs assistance from the teacher and/or a peer in completing the work. It can be difficult for her if there is group work in a class as it can be difficult for her to keep track of or use materials and she tends to be very quiet and not say anything or ask question so that she does not appear to be "stupid" to her peers. Yumi does not read Braille but she does use books on tape for her academic work.

Yumi is pretty shy and generally keeps to herself at school as well as after school and on the weekends. She lives with her parents and does not have any siblings. She enjoys listening to music, cooking (she and her father like to prepare elaborate meals together) and listening to books on tape (biographies of famous women, historical fiction, and young adult literature). Yumi and her mother like to go on walks in the neighborhood and hikes along the beach near their house.

Case Study Evaluation Guided Practice

Below are the areas to assess based upon best practices in inclusive education for students with disabilities. Not all the areas listed may apply to this case study. However, it is important to consider all of them in analyzing academic and support needs and then determining how to successfully build and implement those supports. It is important to have a positive vision of the future for the person, to be comprehensive, and to be creative.

Consider the Following Areas in this Case Study

Accommodations
Modifications
Instructional Strategies
Supports for Teacher
Support for Peers
Support for Family
Positive Behavior Supports
Social Supports
Social Skills Instruction
Self-Management Strategies
Self-Advocacy
Self-Determination
Person-Centered Planning
Inclusion Outside of the Classroom in the School
Inclusion Outside of the School Setting
Executive Functioning
Use of Technology
Physical, Medical, Psychological, or Mental Health Issues
Collaboration
Legal Issues

CASE STUDY NINE: Curt

Case Study Covers:

- *Deaf-Blindness*
- *High School*

Curt is a 15-year-old young man who is deaf and blind. He engages in head hitting, will strike out at others, and throw things that he is handed. Curt has been in a non-public school that services only students diagnosed as having "moderate/severe disabilities." The staff at the school describe Curt as "low functioning" and complain about how he can't learn anything that they try to teach him. In the classroom Curt prefers to sit and rock and flap his hands so that they gently brush against his face. The classroom staff have tried using hand over hand prompts to get him to do tasks, but Curt is often quite resistant to these prompts and will throw things, and if staff persist he will start hitting his head with his fist. Staff usually give up at this point and terminate the instruction. Curt then goes back to his rocking and hand flapping.

Curt's parents are not happy with the program at the school and they decide that they want him to attend the local high school (that is only a few blocks from their house) in the fall when he will be a freshman. They are not sure what type of program that he needs, but they do not believe that his current program is teaching Curt skills that are useful to him and that he is not integrated into his community at all. They are concerned about what his future life will be like if he continues on his current path. They contact the state's Disability Rights Council and talk with an attorney there about the situation. The attorney attends Curt's IEP meeting and the district agrees to have a consultant come and look at the program and make recommendations for an inclusive program at the school.

The consultant, Dr. Grobnik, first meets with the high school staff and they are very skeptical about Curt attending their school, let alone being included into classes and activities at the school. They point out his lack of functional skills for the high school environment, the severity of his disabilities, and his inability to take in information visually or auditorily.

When Dr. Grobnik meets with Curt, his parents, and his two older sisters (one in college and one in high school) he gets a different perspective on the situation. His family members talk about how sweet he is, how he likes interacting with others, his appreciation of good food (his family members like to cook and are "foodies"), and that he has started going with his father to the gym where they life weights together and that has been enjoying the workouts there. They understand his challenging behavior and learning difficulties and why the staff are reluctant to have him attend the high school but they want him to have the chance to be successful in an inclusive educational program and that it may enhance his future life in a positive way.

Case Study Evaluation Guided Practice

Below are the areas to assess based upon best practices in inclusive education for students with disabilities. Not all the areas listed may apply to this case study. However, it is important to consider all of them in analyzing academic and support needs and then determining how to successfully build and implement those supports. It is important to have a positive vision of the future for the person, to be comprehensive, and to be creative.

Consider the Following Areas in this Case Study

Accommodations
Modifications
Instructional Strategies
Supports for Teacher
Support for Peers
Support for Family
Positive Behavior Supports
Social Supports
Social Skills Instruction

Self-Management Strategies
Self-Advocacy
Self-Determination
Person-Centered Planning
Inclusion outside of the Classroom in the School
Inclusion Outside of the School Setting
Executive Functioning
Use of Technology
Physical, Medical, Psychological, or Mental Health Issues
Collaboration
Legal Issues

CASE STUDY TEN: Norma

Case Study Covers:

- *Orthopedic Impairment and Other Health Impairment*
- *High School*

Norma is a 17-year-old high school junior. Norma is outgoing, opinionated, and engaging, and quite feisty. She has cerebral palsy (spasticity with very tight muscles occurring in her arms and legs that result in stiff, uncoordinated movements). Norma also has epilepsy where she has Myoclonic seizures (her muscles suddenly jerk as if Norma has been shocked). Norma also gets tired pretty quickly during the day and also after having a seizure.

Norma moves down the hallways of her high school in her electric wheelchair, greeting peers and teachers. She jokes with them and has an infectious laugh that gets others to join in with her. Norma and her family have recently moved to the town and the school and peers are new to her. She currently does not have a strong social network of friends and does not have an active social life. She has not yet joined any clubs at school and is not involved with any organizations in her community.

There is nobody else like her at school and she is quite different from most of the students that teachers are used to having in their classes. Norma's wheelchair is quite large and this has necessitated the rearrangement of some classroom environments which has not gone over well with some teachers. In addition to difficulties maneuvering around the classroom, Norma also has challenges in navigating school hallways as they are filled with students and staff during passing periods and it can be difficult for Norma to navigate through the crowds to her classes.

In the cafeteria Norma eats off a raised table which makes her stand out. Also, due to her physical impairments she prefers to bring food items from home, and these are things that don't require a lot of utensil use as their use can be difficult for her.

Norma's peers have initially been a bit reluctant to initiate interactions with her as they can be intimated by her using a wheelchair and also because her speech can be hard to understand due to her cerebral palsy, especially in noisy environments such as the cafeteria, quad, and hallways.

Norma has an IEP and she has a variety of specialists involved in developing and implementing an appropriate educational program for her. These specialists include a Physical Therapist who works on gross motor skills, an Occupational Therapists who works on fine motor skills, a Speech-Language Pathologist who work with Norma on her speech and articulation, and an Adapted Physical Education Teacher who works with Norma on different exercise programs. Academically, Norma gets good grades though when she has a seizure or gets tired it can be difficult for her to concentrate or do work. Physically handling papers is difficult for Norma and the teacher or a peer has to help her position the paper on her desk and she prefers to use a voice to text software program for her written work in class.

Case Study Evaluation Guided Practice

Below are the areas to assess based upon best practices in inclusive education for students with disabilities. Not all the areas listed may apply to this case study. However, it is important to consider all of them in analyzing academic and support needs and then determining how to successfully build and implement those supports. It is important to have a positive vision of the future for the person, to be comprehensive, and to be creative.

Consider the Following Areas in this Case Study

Accommodations
Modifications
Instructional Strategies
Supports for Teacher
Support for Peers
Support for Family

Positive Behavior Supports
Social Supports
Social Skills Instruction
Self-Management Strategies
Self-Advocacy
Self-Determination
Person-Centered Planning
Inclusion outside of the Classroom in the School
Inclusion Outside of the School Setting
Executive Functioning
Use of Technology
Physical, Medical, Psychological, or Mental Health Issues
Collaboration
Legal Issues

Appendix A

GENERAL REFERENCES RELATED TO INCLUSION FOR STUDENTS WITH DISABILITIES

BOOKS

Balcazar, F. E. (2010). *Race, culture, and disability: Rehabilitation science and practice.* Sudbury, MA: Jones and Bartlett.

Bauby, J. D. (1997). *The diving bell and the butterfly.* New York: Knopf.

Bell, C. M. (2012). *Blackness and disability: Critical examinations and cultural interventions.* East Lansing, MI: Michigan State University Press.

Bender, K. (2000). *Like normal people.* Boston, MA: Houghton Mifflin.

Berube, M. (1996). *Life as we know it: A father, family, and an exceptional child.* Westminster, MD: Vintage Books.

Bolt, S. E., & Roach, A. T. (2009). *Inclusive assessment and accountability: A guide to accommodations for students with diverse needs.* New York: Guilford Press.

Boon, R. T., & Spencer, V. G. (2010). *Best practices for the inclusive classroom: Scientifically based strategies for success.* Waco, TX: Prufrock Press.

Bragg, B. (1989). *Lessons in laughter: The autobiography of a deaf actor.* Washington DC: Gallaudet University Press.

Browder, D. M., & Spooner, F. (2006). *Teaching language arts, math, and science to students with significant cognitive disabilities.* Baltimore, MD: Paul Brookes.

Browder, D. M., & Spooner, F. (2014). *More language arts, math, and science for students with severe disabilities.* Baltimore, MD: Paul Brookes.

Brown, C. (1970). *Down all the days.* New York: Stein and Day.

Bruinius, H. (2006). *Better for all the world: The secret history of forced sterilization and America's quest for racial purity.* New York: Knopf.

Buchman, D. (2006). *A special education: One family's journey through the maze of learning disabilities.* Cambridge, MA: Da Capo Press Lifelong.

Bumb, P. A. (1996). *My college ring between my toes.* Mansfield, OH: M.C. Bumb.

Burrello, L., Kleinhammer-Tramil, J., & Sailor. W. (2013). *Unifying education systems.* New York, NY: Routledge/Taylor and Francis Group.

Callahan, J. (1990). *Don't worry: He won't get far on foot.* New York: Vintage Press.

Campbell, F. K. (2009). *Contours of ableism: The production of disability and abledness.* New York: Palgrave Macmillan.

Carter, E. W., Cushing, L. S., & Kennedy, C. H. (2009). *Peer support strategies: Improving all students' social lives and learning.* Baltimore, MD: Paul H. Brookes.

Cartledge, G., Gardner, R., & Ford, D. Y. (2009). *Diverse learners with exceptionalities: Culturally responsive teaching in the inclusive classroom.* Upper Saddle River, NJ: Pearson.

Charlton, J. I. (1997). *Nothing about us without us: Disability oppression and empowerment.* Berkeley, CA: University of California Press.

Chivers, S., & Markotic, N. (2010). *The problem body: Projecting disability on film.* Columbus, OH: Ohio State University Press.

Colker, R. (2009). *When is separate unequal?: A disability perspective.* Cambridge, NY: Cambridge University Press.

Davis, L. J. (2017). *The disability studies reader* (5th ed.). New York: Routledge.

Day, P. (2009). *What is friendship?: Games and activities to help children to understand friendship.* Philadelphia, PA: Jessica Kingsley Publishers.

Denecke, J. (2008). *Walking isn't everything: An account of the life of Jean Denecke.* Oshawa, ON: Multi-Media Publications Inc.

Derrida, J. (1993). *Memoirs of the blind: The self-portrait and other ruins.* Chicago: University of Chicago Press.

Dileo, D. (2007). *Raymond's room: Ending the segregation of people with disabilities.* St. Augustine, FL: Training Resources Network.

Espling, L. P. (1997). *Expect the unexpected: My dreams and how I got there.* St. Augustine, FL: Training Resource Network.

Evans, S. E. (2004). *Forgotten crimes: The holocaust and people with disabilities.* Chicago, IL: Ian Dee.

Fiedler, L. (1978). *Freaks.* New York: Simon and Schuster.

Fleischer, D. Z., & Zames, F. (2011). *The disability rights movement: From charity to confrontation.* Philadelphia, Temple University Press.

Fleming, M. (1985). *Images of madness: The portrayal of insanity in the feature film.* Rutherford, NJ: Fairleigh Dickinson University Press.

Friend, M., & Bursuck, W. (2019). *Including students with special needs: A practical guide for classroom teachers* (8th ed.). Upper Saddle River, NJ: Pearson.

Friend, M., & Cook, L. (2020). *Interactions: Collaboration skills for school professionals* (9th ed.). Upper Saddle River, NJ: Pearson.

Fries, K. (1997). *Staring back: The disability experience from the inside out.* New York: Plume

Fries, K. (1997). *Body, remember.* New York: Plume

Gabel, S. I., & Connor, D. J. (2014). *Disability and teaching.* New York: Routledge.

Gallagher, H. G. (1985). *FDR's Splendid Deception.* New York: Dodd, Mead and Company.

Gannon, J. (1981). *Deaf heritage: A narrative history of deaf America.* Washington, DC: National Association of the Deaf.

Gartner, A., & Joe, T. (1987). *Images of the disabled, disabling images.* New York: Praeger.

Ghaly, M. (2010). *Islam and disability: Perspectives in theology and jurisprudence.* New York, NY: Routledge.

Goodey, C. F. (2016). *Learning disability and inclusion phobia: Past, present, future.* New York, NY: Routledge.

Gould, S. J. (2008). *The mismeasure of man.* New York: W.W. Norton.

Grandin, T. (1995). *Thinking in pictures and other reports from my life with autism.* New York: Doubleday.

Grandin, T., & Scariano, M. M. (1986). *Emergence: Labeled autistic: A true story.* NY: Warner Books.

Grassi, E. A., & Barker, H. B. (2010). *Culturally and linguistically diverse exceptional students: Strategies for teaching and assessment.* Los Angeles: Sage.

Grealy, L. (1994). *Autobiography of a face.* Boston: Houghton Mifflin.

Green, S. L. (2014). *S.T.E.M. education: Strategies for teaching learners with special needs.* Hauppauge, NY: Nova Science Publisher's, Inc.

Gregory, G. H., & Chapman, C. (2013). *Differentiated instructional strategies.* Thousand Oaks, CA: Sage, Publications.

Gregory, G. H., & Kuzmich, L. (2014). *Data driven differentiation in the standards-based classroom.* Thousand Oaks, CA: Sage Publications.

Groce, N. (1985). *Everyone here spoke sign language: Hereditary deafness on Martha's Vineyard.* Cambridge, MA: Harvard University Press.

Gronseth, S. L., & Dalton, E. M. (2020). *Universal access through inclusive instructional design: International perspectives on UDL.* New York: Routledge, Taylor & Francis Group.

Grunwald, H. (1999). *Twilight: Losing sight, gaining insight.* New York: Knopf.

Halverson, A. T., & Neary, T. (2009). *Building inclusive schools: Tools and strategies for success* (2nd ed.). Upper Saddle River, NJ: Pearson.

Handler, L. (1998). *Twitch and shout: A Touretter's tale.* New York: Dutton.

Harry, B., & Klingner, J. (2014). *Why are so many minority students in special education?: Understanding race and disability in schools.* New York: Teachers College Press.

Hastings, J. A. (1999). *Voices in the storm: A personal journey of recovery from mental illness.* St. Augustine, FL: Training Resource Network.

Hathaway, K. B. (2000). *The little locksmith: A memoir.* New York: The Feminist Press.

Hendrickx, S. (2009). *The adolescent and adult neuro-diversity handbook: Asperger Syndrome, ADHD, Dyslexia, Dyspraxia and related conditions.* Philadelphia, PA: Jessica Kingsley Publishers.

Herrmann, D. (1998). *Helen Keller: A life.* New York: Knopf.

Hodkinson, A. (2019). *Key issues in special educational needs and inclusion* (3rd ed.). Los Angeles: Sage.

Howell, M., & Ford, P. (1980). *The true history of the elephant man.* New York: Penguin Books.

Hunt, N. (1967). *The world of Nigel Hunt: The diary of a mongoloid.* New York: Garett.

Janney, R., & Snell, M. E. (2013). *Modifying schoolwork* (3rd ed.). Baltimore, MD: Paul H. Brookes.

Janney, R., & Snell, M. E. (2008). *Social relationships and peer support* (2nd ed.). Baltimore, MD: Paul H. Brookes.

Jorgensen, C. M., McSheehan, M., & Sonnenmeier, R. M. (2009). *Promoting membership, participation, and learning for students with disabilities in the general education classroom.* Baltimore, MD: Paul H. Brookes.

Jorgensen, C. M., Schuh, M. C., & Nisbet, J. (2006). *The inclusion facilitator's guide.* Baltimore, MD: Paul H. Brookes.

Johnson, M. (2003). *Make them go away: Clint Eastwood, Christopher Reeve & the case against disability rights.* Louisville, KY: Advocado Press.

Karten, T., J. (2009). *Inclusion strategies that work for adolescent learners!* Thousand Oaks, CA: Corwin Press.

Keller, H. (1903/2003). *The story of my life.* New York: W. W. Norton.

King-Sears, M. E., Janney, R., & Snell, M. E. (2015). *Collaborative teaming* (3rd ed.). Baltimore, MD: Paul Brookes.

Knackendoffel, A., Dettmer, P., & Thurston, L. P., (2017). *Collaboration, consultation, and teamwork for students with special needs* (8th ed.). Boston, MA: Pearson.

Kochhar-Bryant, C. A. (2010). *Effective collaboration for educating the whole child.* Thousand Oaks, CA: Corwin Press.

Lane, H. (1984). *When the mind hears: A history of the Deaf.* New York: Random House.

Lane, H. (1984). *The Deaf experience: Classics in language and education.* Cambridge, MA: Harvard University Press.

Levine, M. D. (1990). *Keeping a head in school.* Cambridge, MA: Educators Publishing Service.

Levine, M. D. (1997). *All kinds of minds.* Cambridge, MA: Educators Publishing Service.

Levine, M. D. (2002). *Educational care: A system for understanding and helping children with learning problems at home and in school* (2nd ed.). Cambridge, MA: Educators Publishing Service.

Levine, M. D., & Reed, M. (1998). *Developmental variation and learning disorders.* Cambridge, MA: Educators Publication Service.

Lewis, R. B., Wheeler, J. J., & Carter, S. L. (2017). *Teaching special students in general education classrooms* (9th ed). Boston, MA: Pearson.

Linton, S. (1998). *Claiming disability: Knowledge and identity.* New York: New York University Press.

Little, J. (1996). *If it weren't for honor—I'd rather have walked: Previously untold tales of the journey to the ADA.* Cambridge, MA: Brookline Books.

Longmore, P. K. (2003). *Why I burned my book and other essays on disability.* Philadelphia, PA: Temple University Press.

Longmore, P. K., & Umansky, L. (2001). *The new disability history: American perspectives.* New York: New York University Press.

Mairs, N. (1998). *Waist-high in the world: A life among the nondisabled.* Boston, MA: Beacon Press.

Malhotra, R., & Rowe, M. (2014). *Exploring disability identity and disability rights through narratives: Finding a voice of their own.* New York, NY: Routledge.

McDonald, D. (2014). *The art of being Deaf: A memoir.* Gallaudet University Press, Washington DC.

McGrath, C. (2007). *The inclusion-classroom problem solver: Structures and supports to serve all learners.* Portsmouth, NH: Heinemann.

McLeskey, J., Rosenberg, M. S., & Westling, D. L. (2009). *Inclusion: Effective practices for all students.* Upper Saddle River, NJ: Pearson.

Mee, C. L. (1999). *A nearly normal life.* Little, Brown, and Company.

Millett, K. (1990). *The loony bin trip.* New York: Simon and Schuster.

Mooney, J. (2007). *The short bus: A journey beyond normal.* New York: Holt.

Murawski, W. W. (2009). *Collaborative teaching in secondary schools: Making the co-teaching marriage work!* Thousand Oaks, CA: Corwin Press.

Murawski, W. W. (2010). *Collaborative teaching in elementary schools: Making the co-teaching marriage work!* Thousand Oaks, CA: Corwin Press.

Myers, H. N., F. (2013). *Social skills deficits in students with disabilities: Successful strategies from the disability field.* Lanham, MD: Rowman & Littlefield Publishers.

Nario-Redmond, M. R. (2020). *Ableism: The causes and consequences of disability prejudice.* Hoboken, NJ: Wiley-Blackwell.

Nielsen, K. E. (2012). *A disability history of the United States.* Boston, MA: Beacon Press.

O'Brien, M. (2003). *How I became a human being: A disabled man's quest for independence.* Madison, WI: University of Wisconsin Press.

Oliver, M. (2009). *Understanding disability: From theory to practice.* New York: Palgrave Macmillan.

Osgood, R. L. (2005). *The history of inclusion in the United States.* Washington, DC: Gallaudet University Press.

Ototake, H. (2000). *No one's perfect.* Tokyo, Japan: Kodansha International.

Panzarino, C. (1994). *The me in the mirror.* Seattle, WA: Seal Press.

Polloway, E. A., Patton, J. R., Serna, L., & Bailey, J. (2018). *Strategies for teaching learners with special needs* (11th ed.). Boston, MA: Pearson.

Prater, M. A., & Dyches, T. T. (2008). *Teaching about disabilities through children's literature.* Westport, CT: Praeger.

Rief, S. F., & Heimburge, J. A. (2006). *How to reach and teach all children in the inclusive classroom: Practical strategies, lessons, and activities* (2nd ed.). San Francisco, CA: Jossey-Bass.

Rose, R., & Shevlin, M. (2010). *Count me in!: Ideas for actively engaging students in inclusive classrooms.* Philadelphia, PA: Jessica Kingsley.

Rothman, D. J. (1984). *The willowbrook wars.* New York: Harper and Row.

Russell, M. (1998). *Beyond ramps: Disability at the end of the social contract.* Monroe, ME: Common Courage Press.

Sailor, W. (2002). *Whole-school success and inclusive education: Building partnerships for learning, achievement, and accountability.* New York: Teachers College Press.

Schillmeier, M. (2010). *Rethinking disability: Bodies, senses and things.* New York: Routledge.

Schiltz, K. L., Schonfeld, A. M., & Niendam, T. (2012). *Beyond the label: A guide to unlocking a child's educational potential.* New York, NY: Oxford University Press.

Shapiro, J. P. (1993). *No pity: People with disabilities forging a new civil rights movement.* New York: Times Books.

Simpson, E. M. (1991). *Reversals: A personal account of victory over Dyslexia.* New York: Farrar, Staus, & Giroux.

Smart, J. (2016). *Disability, society, and the individual* (3rd ed.). Austin, TX: Pro-Ed.

Smith, P. (2013). *Both sides of the table: Autoethnographies of educators learning and teaching with/in disability.* NY: Peter Lang.

Smith, P. (2014). *Disability and diversity: An introduction.* Dubuque, IA: Kendall Hunt Publishing.

Smith, T. (2011). *Making inclusion work for students with Autism Spectrum Disorders: An evidence-based guide.* New York: Guilford.

Smith, T. E. C., Gartin, B. C., & Murdick, N. L. (2012). *Including adolescents with disabilities in general education classrooms.* Boston, MA: Pearson.

Stroman, D. F. (2003). *The disability rights movement: From deinstitutionalization to self-determination.* Lanham, MD: University Press of America.

Sullivan, T., & Gill, D. (1975). *If you could see what I hear.* New York: New American Library.

Valle, J. W., & Connor, D. J. (2019). *Rethinking disability: A disability studies approach to inclusive practices* (2nd ed.). New York: Routledge.

Vaughn, S., Bos, C. S., & Schumm, J. S. (2018). *Teaching students who are exceptional, diverse, and at risk in the general education classroom* (7th ed.). Boston: Merrill.

Villa, R. A., & Thousand, J. S. (2005). *Creating an inclusive school* (2nd ed.). Alexandria, VA: Association for Supervision and Curriculum Development.

Villa, R. A., & Thousand, J. S. (2016). *Leading an inclusive school* (2nd ed.). Alexandria, VA: Association for Supervision and Curriculum Development.

Villa, R. A., Thousand, J. S., & Nevin, A. I. (2013). *A guide to co-teaching: Practical tips for facilitating student learning* (3rd ed.). Thousand Oaks, CA: Corwin Press.

Volpe, R. J., & Fabiano, G. A. (2013). *Daily behavior report cards: An evidence-based system of assessment and intervention.* New York: The Guilford Press.

West, T. G. (1991). *In the mind's eye: Visual thinkers, gifted people with learning difficulties, computer images, and the ironies of creativity.* Buffalo, NY: Prometheus Books.

Wilkerson, K. L., Perzigian, A. B. T., & Schurr, J. K. (2014). *Promoting social skills in the inclusive classroom.* New York: Guilford Press.

Williams, D. (1992). *Nobody nowhere: The extraordinary autobiography of an autistic.* New York: Times Books.

Williams, D. (1994). *Somebody somewhere: Breaking free from the world of autism.* New York: Times Books.

Williams, D. (1996). *Like color to the blind.* New York: Times Books.

Wilson, G. L., & Blednick, J. (2011). *Teaching in tandem: Effective coteaching in the inclusive classroom.* Alexandria, VA: ASCD.

JOURNAL ARTICLES

Agran, M., Alper, S., & Wehmeyer, M. (2002). Access to the general education curriculum for students with significant disabilities: What it means for teachers. *Education and Training in Mental Retardation and Developmental Disabilities, 37,* 123–133.

Ashby, C., Burns, J., & Royle, J. (2014). ALL kids can be readers: the marriage of reading first and inclusive education. *Theory into Practice, 53,* 98–105.

Ayala, E. C. (1999). "Poor little things" and "brave little souls": The portrayal of individuals with disabilities in children's literature. *Research and Instruction, 39,* 103–117.

Ballard, S. L., & Dymond, S. K. (2019). Inclusive education for secondary age students with severe disabilities and complex health care needs. *Intellectual and Developmental Disabilities, 56,* 427–441.

Basham, J. D., & Marino, M. T. (2013). Understanding STEM education and supporting students through universal design for learning. *Teaching Exceptional Children, 45*(4), 8–15.

Bay-Hinitz, A. K., Peterson, R. F., & Qualitch, H. R. (1994). Cooperative games: A way to modify aggressive and cooperative behaviors in young children. *Journal of Applied Behavior Analysis, 27,* 435–446.

Boyle, J. R. (2001). Enhancing the note-taking skills of students with mild disabilities. *Intervention in School and Clinic, 36,* 221–222.

Brock, M. E., Biggs, E. E., Carter, E. W., Cattey, G., & Raley, K. (2016). Implementation and generalization of peer support arrangements for students with significant disabilities in inclusive classrooms. *The Journal of Special Education, 49,* 221–232.

Brown, L., Schwarz, P., Udvari-Solner, A., Kampschroer, E. F., Johnson, F., Jorgensen, J., & Gruenewald, L. (1991). How much time should students with severe intellectual disabilities spend in regular education classrooms and elsewhere? *Journal of the Association for Persons with Severe Handicaps, 16,* 39–47.

Brown, L., Udvari-Solner, A., Schwarz, P., VanDeventer, P., Ahlgren, C., Johnson, F., Gruenewald, L., & Jorgensen, J., (1989). Should students with severe intellectual disabilities be based in regular or in special education classrooms in home schools? *Journal of the Association for Persons with Severe Handicaps, 14,* 8–12.

Carnahan, C. R., Williamson, P., Clarke, L., & Sorensen, R. (2009). A systematic approach for supporting paraeducators in educational settings: A guide for teachers. *Teaching Exceptional Children, 41,* 34–45.

Carter, E. W., Asmus, J., Moss, C. K., Cooney, M., Weir, K., Vincent, L., Born, T., Hochman, J., Bottema-Beutel, K., & Fesperman, E. (2013). Peer network strategies to foster social connections among adolescents with and without severe disabilities. *Teaching Exceptional Children, 46*(2), 51–59.

Carter, E. W., Cushing, L. S., Clark, N. M., & Kennedy, C. H. (2005). Effects of peer support interventions on students' access to the general curriculum and social interactions. *Research and Practice for Persons with Severe Disabilities, 30,* 15–25.

Carter, E. W., Common, E. A., Sreckovic, M. A., Huber, H. B., Bottema-Beutel, K., Gustafson, J. R., Dykstra, J., & Hume, K. (2014). Promoting social competence and peer relationships for adolescents with ASD. *Remedial and Special Education, 35,* 27–37.

Carter, E. W., Moss, C. K., Asmus, J., Fesperman, E., Cooney, M., Brock, M. E., Lyons, G., Huber, H. B., & Vincent, L. B. (2015). Promoting inclusion, social relationships, and learning through peer support arrangements. *Teaching Exceptional Children, 48*(1), 9–18.

Carter, E. W., Swedeen, B., Moss, C. K., & Pesko, M. J. (2010). "What are you doing after school?" Promoting extracurricular involvement for transition-age youth with disabilities. *Intervention in School and Clinic, 45,* 275–283.

Cartledge, G., & Kourea, L. (2008). Culturally responsive classrooms for culturally diverse students with and at risk for disabilities. *Exceptional Children, 74,* 351-371.

Causton-Theoharis, J. N. (2010). The golden rule of providing support in inclusive classrooms: Support others as you would wish to be supported. *Teaching Exceptional Individuals, 42,* 36–43.

Copeland, S. R., & Hughes, C. (2002). Effects of goal setting on task performance of persons with mental retardation. *Education and Training in Mental Retardation and Developmental Disabilities, 37,* 40–54.

Cornelius, K. E. (2013). Formative assessment made easy: Templates for collecting daily data in inclusive classrooms. *Teaching Exceptional Children, 45*(5), 14–21.

Darig, J. C. (2005). The McClurg monthly magazine and 14 more practical ways to involve parents. *Teaching Exceptional Children, 38,* 46–51.

Davern, L., & Schnorr, R. (1992). Public schools welcome students with disabilities as full members. *Children Today, 20,* 21–25.

Denti, L. G., & Meyers, S. B. (1997). Successful ability awareness programs: The key is in the planning. *Teaching Exceptional Children, 29,* 52–54.

Deshler, D., Schumaker, J., Bulgren, J., Lenz, K., Jantzen, J.-E., Adams, G., Carnine, D., Grossen, B., Davis, B., & Marquis, J. (2001). Making learning easier: Connecting new knowledge to things students already know. *Teaching Exceptional Children, 33,* 82–85.

Doyle, M. B. & Giangreco, M. F. (2013). Guiding principles for including high school students with intellectual disabilities in general education classes. *American Secondary Education, 42*(1), 57–72.

Falkenberg, C., & Barbetta, P. (2013). The effects of a self-monitoring package on homework completion and accuracy of students with disabilities in an inclusive general education classroom. *Journal of Behavioral Education, 22,* 190–210.

Fenty, N. S., McDuffie-Landrum, K., & Fisher, G. (2012). Using collaboration, co-teaching, and question answer relationships to enhance content area literacy. *Teaching Exceptional Children, 44*(6), 28–37.

Fisher, D., & Frey, N. (2001). Access to the core curriculum: Critical ingredients for student success. *Remedial and Special Education, 22,* 148–157.

Ford, D. Y. (2012). Culturally different students in special education: Looking backward to move forward. *Exceptional Children, 78,* 391–405.

Fryxell, D., & Kennedy, C. H. (1995). Placement along the continuum of services and its impact on students' social relationships. *Journal of the Association for Persons with Severe Handicaps, 20,* 259–269.

Fuchs, D., & Fuchs, L. S. (1995). What's 'special' about special education? *Phi Delta Kappan, 76,* 522–530.

Fuchs, L. S., & Fuchs, D. (1998). General educators' instructional adaptations for students with learning disabilities. *Learning Disability Quarterly, 21,* 23–33.

Fuchs, D., Fuchs, L.S., & Vaughn, S.R. (2014). What is intensive instruction and why is it important? *Teaching Exceptional Children, 46,* 13–18.

Giangreco, M. F. (2010). One-to-one paraprofessionals for students with disabilities in inclusive classrooms: Is conventional wisdom wrong? *Intellectual and Developmental Disabilities, 48,* 1–13.

Giangreco, M. F., Broer, S. M., & Edelman, S. W. (1999). The tip of the iceberg: Determining whether paraprofessional support is needed for students with disabilities in general education settings. *Journal of the Association for Persons with Severe Handicaps, 24,* 281–291.

Giangreco, M. F., Broer, S. M., & Edelman, S. W. (2001). Paraprofessional support of students with disabilities: Literature from the past decade. *Exceptional Children, 68,* 45–63.

Giangreco, M., Dennis, R., Cloninger, C., Edelman, S., & Schattman, R. (1993). "I've counted Jon": Transformational experiences of teachers educating students with disabilities. *Exceptional Children, 59,* 359–372.

Giangreco, M. F., Doyle, M. B., & Suter, J. C. (2012). Constructively responding to requests for paraprofessionals: We keep asking the wrong questions. *Remedial and Special Education, 33,* 362–373.

Giangreco, M. F., Yuan, S., McKenzie, B., Cameron, P., & Fialka, J. (2005). "Be careful what you wish for . . .": Five reasons to be concerned about the assignment of individual paraprofessionals. *Teaching Exceptional Children, 37,* 28–34.

Gilson, S. F., & Depoy, E. (2000). Multiculturalism and disability: A critical perspective. *Disability & Society, 15,* 207–218.

Haring, T. G., & Breen, C. G. (1992). A peer-mediated social network intervention to enhance the social integration of persons with moderate and severe disabilities. *Journal of Applied Behavior Analysis, 25,* 319–333.

Harn, B. A., Chard, D. J., Biancarosa, G., & Kame'enui, E. J. (2011). Coordinating instructional supports to accelerate at-risk first grade readers performance: An essential mechanism for effective RtI. *Elementary School Journal, 112*(2), 332–355.

Harris, K. R., Graham, S., Friedlander, B., & Laud, L. (2013). Bring powerful writing strategies into your classroom! *Why and how. Reading Teacher, 66,* 538–542.

Harrower, J. K., & Dunlap, G. (2001). Including students with autism in general education classrooms: A review of effective strategies. *Behavior Modification, 25,* 762–784.

Harry, B. (2008). Collaboration with culturally and linguistically diverse families: Ideal versus reality. *Exceptional Children, 74,* 372–388.

Heward, W. L. (2003). Ten faulty notions about teaching and learning that hinder the effectiveness of special education. *Journal of Special Education, 36,* 186–205.

Hughes, C., Copeland, S. R., Agran, M., Wehmeyer, M. L., Rodi, M. S., & Presley, J. A. (2002). Using self-monitoring to improve performance in general education high school classes. *Education and Training in Mental Retardation and Developmental Disabilities, 37,* 262–272.

Israel, M., Maynard, K., & Williamson, P. (2013). Promoting literacy-embedded, authentic STEM instruction for students with disabilities and other struggling learners. *Teaching Exceptional Children, 45*(4), 18–25.

Janney, R. E., Snell, M. E., Beers, M. K., & Raynes, M. (1995). Integrating students with moderate and severe disabilities into general education classes. *Exceptional Children, 61,* 425–439.

Janney, R. E., & Snell, M. E. (1996). How teachers use peer interactions to include students with moderate and severe disabilities in elementary general education classes. *Journal of the Association for Persons with Severe Handicaps, 21,* 72–80.

Knight, V. F., Spooner, F., Browder, D. M., Smith, B. R., & Wood, C. L. (2013). Using graphic organizers and systematic instruction to teach science concepts to students with autism spectrum disorder. *Focus on Autism and Other Developmental Disabilities, 42,* 378–389.

Koegel, L. K., Harrower, J. K., & Koegel, R. L. (1999). Support for children with developmental disabilities in full inclusion classrooms through self-management. *Journal of Positive Behavior Interventions, 1,* 26–34.

Kuntz, E. M., & Carter, E. W. (2019). Review of interventions supporting secondary students with intellectual disability in general education classes. *Research and Practice for Persons with Severe Disabilities, 44,* 103–121.

Kurth, J. A. (2013). A unit-based approach to adaptations in inclusive classrooms. *Teaching Exceptional Children, 46,* 34–43.

Lalvani, P., & Broderick, A. (2013). Institutionalized ableism and the misguided "disability awareness day": Transformative pedagogies for teacher education. *Equity and Excellence in Education, 46,* 468–483.

Learned, J. E., Dowd, M. V., & Jenkins, J. R. (2009). Instructional conferencing: Helping students succeed on independent assignments in inclusive settings. *Teaching Exceptional Children, 41,* 46–51.

Lee, S. J., Wehmeyer, M. L., Soukup, J. H., & Palmer, S. B. (2010), Impact of curriculum modifications on access to the general education curriculum for students with disabilities. *Exceptional Children, 76,* 213–233.

Lemons, C. J., Kearns, D. M., & Davidson, K. A. (2014). Data-based individualization in reading. *Teaching Exceptional Children, 46,* 20–29.

Lipsky, D. K., & Gartner, A. (1996). Inclusion, school restructuring, and the remaking of American society. *Harvard Educational Review, 66,* 762–796.

Logan, K. R., & Malone, D. M. (1998). Comparing instructional contexts of students with and without severe disabilities in general education classes. *Exceptional Children, 64,* 343–358.

Longmore, P. K. (1995). The second phase: From disability rights to disability culture. *The Disability Rag & Resource, 16*(5), 4–11.

Ming, K., & Dukes, C. (2008). Fluency: A necessary ingredient in comprehensive reading instruction in inclusive classrooms. *Teaching Exceptional Children Plus, 4*(4).

Morgan, P. L., Young, C., & Fuchs, D. (2006). Peer-assisted learning strategies: An effective intervention for young readers. *Insights on Learning Disabilities, 3,* 23–41.

Mortier, K. (2020). Communities of practice: A conceptual framework for inclusion of students with significant disabilities. *International Journal of Inclusive Education, 24,* 329–340.

Murphy, D. M. (1996). Implications of inclusion for general and special education. *The Elementary School Journal, 96,* 469–493.

Obiakor, F. E., Harris, M., Mutua, K., Rotatori, A., & Algozzine, B. (2012). Making inclusion work in general education classrooms. *Education and Treatment of Children, 35,* 477–490.

Pomplun, M. (1997). When students with disabilities participate in cooperative groups. *Exceptional Children, 64,* 49–58.

Prater, M. A. (1999). Characterization of mental retardation in children's and adolescent literature. *Education and Training in Mental Retardation and Developmental Disabilities, 34,* 418–431.

Saunders, A., Bethune, K. S., Spooner, F., & Browder, D. B. (2013). Solving the Common Core equation: An approach to teaching Common Core Mathematics Standards to students with moderate and severe disabilities. *Teaching Exceptional Children, 45*(3), 24–33.

Shukla, S., Kennedy, C. H. & Cushing, L. S. (1999). Intermediate school students with severe disabilities: Supporting their social participation in general education classrooms. *Journal of Positive Behavior Interventions, 1,* 130–140.

Turner, S., Alborz, A., & Gayle, V. (2008). Predictors of academic attainments of young people with Down's syndrome. *Journal of Intellectual Disability Research, 52,* 380–392.

Van Dyke, R., Stallings, M. A., & Colley, K. (1995). How to build an inclusive school community. *Phi Delta Kappa, 76,* 475–479.

Vaughn, S., Elbaum, B. E., & Schumm, J. S. (1996). The effects of inclusion on the social functioning of students with learning disabilities. *Journal of Learning Disabilities, 29,* 598–608.

Vaughn, S., & Linan-Thompson, S. (2003). What is special about special education for students with Learning Disabilities? *Journal of Special Education, 37,* 140–147.

Watt, S. J., Therrien, W. J., Kaldenberg, E., & Taylor, J. (2013). Promoting inclusive practices in inquiry-based science classrooms. *Teaching Exceptional Children, 45*(4), 40–48.

Wehmeyer, M. L., Lance, G. D., & Bashinski, S. (2002). Promoting access to the general curriculum for students with mental retardation: A multi-level model. *Education and Training in Mental Retardation and Developmental Disabilities, 37,* 223–234.

Whitby, P. J. S., Leininger, M. L., & Grillo, K. (2012). Tips for using interactive whiteboards to increase participation of students with disabilities. *Teaching Exceptional Children, 44*(6), 50–57.

Appendix B

ORGANIZATIONS AND RESOURCES
REGARDING INCLUSION AND DISABILITY

JOURNALS AND RESOURCES

General, Public Policy and Legal

Journals

Disability and Society
Disability Studies Quarterly
Education and Treatment of Children
Educational Evaluation and Policy Analysis
Educational Policy
Exceptional Children
Exceptionality
Inclusion
Journal of Disability Policy Studies
Journal of International Special Needs Education
Journal of Special Education
Journal of Special Education Leadership
Remedial and Special Education
Rural Special Education Quarterly Journal
Teacher Education and Special Education

Resources

Council for Exceptional Children
3100 Clarendon Blvd, Suite 600
Arlington, VA 22201-5332
888-232-7733
service@cec.sped.org
www.cec.sped.org

National Disability Rights Network
820 1st Street NE, Suite 740
Washington, DC 20002
202/408-9514
www.ndm.org
info@ndm.org

National Council on Disability
1331 F Street, NW, Suite 850
Washington, DC 20004
202/272-2004
www.ncd.gov
ncd@ncd.gov

American Council on Rural Special Education
West Virginia University
509 Allen Hall, PO Box 6122
Morgantown, WV 26506-6122
304-293-3450
acres-sped@mail.wvu.edu
www.acres-sped.org

Society for Disability Studies
The City University of New York
101 W. 31st Street (12th floor)
New York, NY 10001
212/652-2005
www.disstudies.org

Disability Rights Education and Defense Fund
3075 Adeline Street, Suite 210
Berkeley, CA 94703
510/644-2555
info@dredf.org
www.dredf.org

National Organization on Disability
77 Water Street, Suite 204
New York, NY 10005
646/505-1191
www.nod.org
info@nod.org

National Association of State Directors of Special Education
1800 Diagonal Road, Suite 600
Alexandria, VA 22314
703/519-3800
www.nasdse.org

Bazelon Center for Mental Health Law
1090 Vermont Avenue, NW, Suite 220
Washington, DC 20005
202/467-5730
www.bazelon.org
communications@bazelon.org

World Institute on Disability
3075 Adeline Street, Suite 155
Berkeley, CA 94703
510/225-6400
www.wid.org
wid@wid.org

Visual Impairments

Journals

Journal of Visual Impairment and Blindness

Resources

American Council of the Blind
1703 N. Beauregard St., Suite 420
Alexandria, VA 22311
800/424-8666
www.acb.org
info@acb.org

National Federation of the Blind
200 East Wells Street
Baltimore, MD 21230
410/659-9314
www.nfb.org
nfb@nfb.org

American Foundation for the Blind
1401 South Clark Street, Suite 730
Arlington, VA 22202
212/502-7600
www.afb.org
afbinfo@afb.net

Learning Disabilities

Journals

Journal of Learning Disabilities
Learning Disabilities Forum
Learning Disabilities Quarterly
Learning Disabilities Research and Practice
Reading and Writing Quarterly: Overcoming Learning Difficulties

Resources

Learning Disabilities Association of America
461 Cochran Road, Suite 245
Pittsburgh, PA 15228
412/341-1515
https://ldaamerica.org
info@LDAAmerica.org

National Institute for Direct Instruction
P.O. Box 11248
Eugene, OR 97440
541/485-1973
info@nifdi.org
https://www.nifdi.org

International Dyslexia Association
40 York Rd., 4th Floor
Baltimore, MD 21204
410/296-0232
www.interdys.org

The Council for Learning Disabilities
11184 Antioch Road
Box 405
Overland Park, KS 66210
913/491-1011
www.cldinternational.org
CLDInfo@ie-events.com

Children and Adults with Attention Deficit Disorders (CHADD)
4221 Forbes Blvd, Suite 270
Lanham, MD 20706
301/306-7070
www.chadd.org

National Center for Learning Disabilities
1 Thomas Circle NW, #700
Washington, DC 20005
www.ncld.org

Communication Disorders

Journals

American Journal of Speech Language Pathology
Augmentative and Alternative Communication
Communication Education
Human Communication Research
Journal of Childhood Communication Disorders
Journal of Communication Disorders
Journal of Speech and Hearing Disorders
Journal of Speech and Hearing Research
Language, Speech and Hearing Services in the Schools
Communication Teacher
Speech and Hearing Services in the Schools
Topics in Language Disorders

Resources

American Speech, Language, and Hearing Association
2200 Research Boulevard
Rockville, MD 20850-3289
800/638-8255
www.asha.org

Stuttering Foundation of America
PO Box 11749
Memphis, TN 38111-0749
800/992-9392
www.stutteringhelp.org
info@stutteringhelp.org

Behavior Disorders/Emotional Disturbance

Journals

Behavior Analysis in Practice
Behavior Modification
Behavior Therapy
Behavioral Disorders
Journal of Applied Behavior Analysis
Journal of Positive Behavior Interventions
Journal of Emotional and Behavioral Disorders

Resources

The Association for Behavior Analysis
550 West Centre Avenue, Suite 1
Portage, MI 49024
269/492-9310
www.abainternational.org
mail@abainternational.org

National Alliance for the Mentally Ill
3803 N. Fairfax Dr., Ste. 100
Arlington, VA 22203
800/950-6264
www.nami.org

Cambridge Center for Behavioral Studies
410 Newtown Road
Littleton, MA 01460
978/369-2227
www.behavior.org

The Association of Positive Behavior Support
P.O Box 328
Bloomsburg, PA 17815
570/441-5418
www.apbs.org
tknoster@bloomu.edu

Deaf Culture/Hearing Impairments

Journals

American Annals of the Deaf
Journal of the American Deafness and Rehabilitation Association
Sign Language Studies

Resources

National Association of the Deaf
8630 Fenton Street, Suite 820
Silver Spring, MD 20910-3876
301/587-1788
www.nad.orgNADinfo@nad.org

Computers and Technology

Journals

Classroom Computer Learning
Computers and Education
Computers in Human Behavior
Computers in Human Services
Computers in the Schools
Journal of Computer Assisted Learning
Journal of Computer-Based Education
Journal of Special Education Technology
Teaching and Computers
Technology and Disability

Resources

Center for Applied Special Technology
200 Harvard Mill Square, Suite 210
781/245-2212
www.cast.org
cast@cast.org

Physical Disabilities

Journals

American Journal of Occupational Therapy
Canadian Journal of Occupational Therapy

Physical and Occupational Therapy in Pediatrics
Physical Disabilities: Education and Related Services
Physical Therapy
Physical Therapy Practice
Adapted Physical Activity Quarterly
Journal of Developmental and Physical Disabilities
Mainstream: Magazine of the Able-Disabled

Resources

United Cerebral Palsy
1825 K Street NW Suite 600
Washington, DC 20006
202/776-0406
www.ucp.org
info@ucp.org

Developmental Disabilities/Intellectual Disabilities

Journals

American Journal on Intellectual and Developmental Disabilities
Journal of Intellectual and Developmental Disability
Education and Training in Autism and Developmental Disabilities
Applied Research in Intellectual Disabilities
Journal of Intellectual Disabilities Research
Journal of Policy and Practice in Intellectual Disabilities
Intellectual and Developmental Disabilities
Research and Practice for Persons with Severe Disabilities
Research in Developmental Disabilities

Resources

TASH
1101 15th Street NW, Suite 206
Washington, D.C. 20005
202/817-3264
www.tash.org

American Association on Intellectual and Developmental Disabilities
8403 Colesville Road, Suite 900
Silver Spring, MD 20910
202/387-1968
www.aaidd.org

The Arc of the United States
1825 K Street NW, Suite 1200
Washington, DC 20006
800/433-5255
www.thearc.org
info@thearc.org

National Down Syndrome Society
8 E 41st Street, 8th Floor
New York, NY 10017
800/221-4602
www.ndss.org
info@ndss.org

International Association for the Scientific Study of Intellectual Disabilities
IASSID Member Affairs Office
Box 671, URMC
601 Elmwood Avenue
Rochester, New York 14642
www.iassid.org
admin@iassidd.org

Parents/Families

Journals

Child and Family Behavior Therapy
Child and Youth Services
Child Study Journal
Contemporary Family Therapy
Families in Society
Family Process
Journal of Child and Family Studies
Journal of Divorce and Remarriage
Journal of Family History
Journal of Family Practice
Journal of Family Psychology
Journal of Family Violence
Journal of Marriage and the Family
Parent
The Exceptional Parent

Resources

Parent Advocacy Coalition for Education Rights
8161 Normandale Blvd.
Minneapolis, MN 55437
952/838-9000
www.pacer.org
pacer@pacer.org

Beach Center on Disability
University of Kansas
Haworth Hall
1200 Sunnyside Avenue, Room 3134
Lawrence, KS 66045-7534
785/864-7600
https://beachcenter.lsi.ku.edu
beachcenter@ku.edu

Autism Spectrum Disorders

Journals

Autism Advocate
Autism Insights
Autism Research and Treatment
Autism Research Review International
Good Autism Practice Journal
Journal of Autism and Developmental Disorders
Focus on Autism and Other Developmental Disabilities
Research in Autism Spectrum Disorders

Resources

Autism Society of America
6110 Executive Boulevard, Suite 305
Rockville, MD 2085
800/328-8476
www.autism-society.org

UC Davis M.I.N.D. Institute
2825 50th Street
Sacramento, CA 95817
916/703-0280
www.ucdmc.ucdavis.edu/mindinstitute

National Autism Association
One Park Avenue, Suite 1
Portsmouth, RI 02871
877/622-2884
www.nationalautismassociation.org
naa@nationalautism.org

Autism Speaks
1 East 33rd Street, 4th Floor
New York, NY 10016
646/385-8500
www.autismspeaks.org
contactus@autismspeaks.org

Miscellaneous

Epilepsy Foundation
8301 Professional Place West, Suite 230
Landover, MD 20785-2356
301/459-3700
www.epilepsy.com
ContactUs@efa.org

Tourette Syndrome Association
42-40 Bell Boulevard, Suite 205
Bayside, NY 11361
www.tourette.org
support@tourette.org

National Association for the Dually Diagnosed
12 Hurley Avenue
Kingston, NY 12401
845/331-4336
www.thenadd.org
info@thenadd.org

Appendix C

EMPIRICAL RESEARCH TO SUPPORT THAT THE INTERVENTIONS USED IN THE CASE STUDIES ARE EVIDENCE-BASED PRACTICES

Accommodations

Baker, D., & Scanlon, D. (2016). Student perspectives on academic accommodations. *Exceptionality, 24,* 93–108.

Feucht, F. C., & Holmgren, C. R. (2018). Developing tactile maps for students with visual impairments: A case study for customizing accommodations. *Journal of Visual Impairment and Blindness, 112,* 143–155.

Fuchs, L. S., & Fuchs, D. (1998). General educators' instructional adaptations for students with learning disabilities. *Learning Disability Quarterly, 21,* 23–33.

Green, J. G., Donaldson, A. R., Nadeau, M. S.; Reid, G., Pincus, D. B., Comer, J. S., & Elkins, R. M. (2017). School functioning and use of school-based accommodations by treatment-seeking anxious children. *Journal of Emotional and Behavioral Disorders, 25,* 220–232.

Joyce, J., Harrison, J. R., & Gitomer, D. H. (2020). Modifications and accommodations: A preliminary investigation into changes in classroom artifact quality. *International Journal of Inclusive Education, 24,* 181–201.

Kern, L., Hetrick, A. A., Custer, B. A., & Commisso, C. E. (2019). An evaluation of IEP accommodations for secondary students with emotional and behavioral problems. *Journal of Emotional and Behavioral Disorders, 27,* 178–192.

Kettler, R. (2012). Testing accommodations: Theory and research to inform practice. *International Journal of Disability, Development and Education, 59,* 53–66.

van Munster, M. A., Lieberman, L. J., & Grenier, M, A. (2019). Universal design for learning and differentiated instruction in physical education. *Adapted Physical Activity Quarterly, 36,* 359–377.

Modifications

Gunter, P. L., Denny, R. K., & Venn, M. L. (2000). Modification of instructional materials and procedures for curricular success of students with emotional and behavioral disorders. *Preventing School Failure, 44,* 116–122.

Hay, G. H., & Courson, F. H. (1997). Strategies for success in inclusive classrooms. *Reading and Writing Quarterly, 13,* 97–100.

Kurth, J. A., & Keegan, L. (2014). Development and use of curricular adaptations for students receiving special education services. *Journal of Special Education, 48,* 191–203.

Lee, S. H., Wehmeyer, M. L., Soukup, J. H., & Palmer, S. B. (2010). Impact of curriculum modifications on access to the general education curriculum for students with disabilities. *Exceptional Children, 76,* 213–233.

Randall, J., & Engelhard, G. (2010). Performance of students with and without disabilities under modified conditions. *Journal of Special Education, 44,* 79–93.

Soukup, J. H., Wehmeyer, M. L., Bashinski, S. M., & Bovaird, J. A. (2007). Classroom variables and access to the general curriculum for students with disabilities. *Exceptional Children, 74,* 101–120.

Zhang, D., Wang, Q., Ding, Y., & Liu, J. J. (2014). Testing accommodation or modification?: The effects of integrated object representation on enhancing geometry performance in children with and without geometry difficulties. *Journal of Learning Disabilities, 47,* 569–583.

Instructural Strategies

Bates, P., Cuvo, T., Miner, C., & Korabek, C. (2001). Simulated and community-based instruction involving persons with mild and moderate mental retardation. *Research in Developmental Disabilities, 22,* 95–115.

Delquardi, J., Greenwood, C. R., Wharton, D., Carta, J. J., & Hall, R. V. (1986). Classwide peer tutoring. *Exceptional Children, 52,* 535–542.

Fuchs, D., Fuchs, L. S., Mathes, P., & Simmons, D. (1997). Peer-Assisted Learning Strategies: Making classrooms more responsive to student diversity. *American Educational Research Journal, 34,* 174–206.

Fuchs, D., Fuchs, L. S., & Burish, P. (2000). Peer-Assisted Learning Strategies: An evidence-based practice to promote reading achievement. *Learning Disabilities Research and Practice, 15,* 85–91.

Haydon, T., Maheady, L., & Hunter, W. (2010). Effects of numbered heads together on the daily quiz scores and on-task behavior of students with disabilities. *Journal of Behavioral Education, 19,* 222–238.

Kuntz, E., & Carter, E. W. (2019). Review of interventions supporting secondary students with intellectual disability in general education classrooms. *Research and Practice for Persons with Severe Disabilities, 44,* 103–121.

Pennington, R. C., & Delano, M. E. (2012). Writing instruction for students with autism spectrum disorders: A review of literature. *Focus on Autism and Other Developmental Disabilities, 27,* 239–248.

Powell, L. E., Glang, A., Ettel, D., Todis, B., Sohlberg, M., & Albin, R. (2012). Systematic instruction for individuals with acquired brain injury: Results of a randomized controlled trial. *Neuropsychological Rehabilitation, 22,* 85–112.

Sears, D. A., & Pai, H. (2012). Effects of cooperative versus individual study on learning and motivation after reward-removal. *Journal of Experimental Education, 80,* 246–262.

Strom, P. S., & Strom, R. D. (2011). Teamwork skills assessment for cooperative learning. *Educational Research and Evaluation, 17,* 233–251.

Zakas, T., Browder, D.M., Ahlgrim-Delzell, L., & Heafner, T. (2013). Teaching social studies to students with autism using a graphic organizer intervention. *Research in Autism Spectrum Disorders, 7,* 1075–1086.

Supports for Teachers

Able, H., Sreckovic, M.A., Schultz, T. R., Garwood, J. D., & Sherman, J. (2015). Views from the trenches: Teacher and student supports needed for full inclusion of students with ASD. *Teacher Education and Special Education, 38,* 44–57.

Biggs, E. E., Gilson, C. B., & Carter, E. W. (2019). "Developing that balance": Preparing and supporting special education teachers to work with paraprofessionals. *Teacher Education and Special Education, 42,* 117–131.

Carnahan, C. R., Williamson, P., Clarke, L., & Sorensen, R. (2009). A systematic approach for supporting paraeducators in educational settings: A guide for teachers. *Teaching Exceptional Children, 41,* 34–45.

Cutter, J., Palincsar, A. S., & Magnusson, S. J. (2002). Supporting inclusion through case-based vignette conversations. *Learning Disabilities Research and Practice, 17,* 186–200.

Eysink, T., Hulsbeek, M., & Gijlers, H. (2017). Supporting primary school teachers in differentiating in the regular classroom. *Teaching and Teacher Education, 66,* 107–116.

Gilbertson, D., Witt, J. C., & Singletary, L. L (2007). Supporting teacher use of intervention: Effects of response dependent performance feedback on teacher implementation of a math intervention. *Journal of Behavioral Education, 16,* 311–326.

Kennedy, E., & Laverick, L. (2019). Leading inclusion in complex systems: Experiences of relational supervision for head teachers. *Support for Learning, 34,* 443–459.

Schlessinger, S. L. (2018). Reclaiming teacher intellectualism through and for inclusive education. *International Journal of Inclusive Education, 22,* 268–284.

Support for Peers

Campbell, J. M. (2007). Middle school students' responses to the self-introduction of a student with autism: Effects of perceived similarity, prior awareness, and education message. *Remedial and Special Education, 28,* 163–173.

Hunt, P., Farron-Davis, F, & Wrenn, M. (1997). Promoting interactive partnerships in inclusive educational settings. *Journal of the Association for Persons with Severe Handicaps, 22,* 127–137.

Kim, J., Park, E., & Snell, M. E. (2005). Impact of information and weekly contact on attitudes orean general educators and nondisabled students regarding peers with disabilities. *Mental Retardation, 43,* 401–415.

Leigers, K., Kleinert, H., & Carter, E. W. (2017). "I never truly thought about them having friends": Equipping schools to foster peer relationships. *Rural Special Education Quarterly, 36,* 73–83.

Lindsay, S., & Edwards, A. (2013). A systematic review of disability awareness interventions for children and youth. *Disability and Rehabilitation, 35,* 623–646.

Staub, D., & Hunt, P (1993). The effects of social interaction training on high school peer tutors of schoolmates with severe disabilities. *Exceptional Children, 60,* 41–57.

Williams, L. J., & Downing, J. E. (1998). Membership and belonging in inclusive classrooms: What do middle school students have to say? *Journal of the Association for Persons with Severe Handicaps, 23,* 98–110.

Support for Families

Bhatia, (2018). Promoting resiliency in families of individuals with disabilities: Role of coping resources, family support, social participation and perceived burden. *Indian Journal of Health and Wellbeing, 9,* 599–608.

Francis, G. L., Blue-Banning, M., Haines, S. J., Turnbull, A.P., & Gross, J. M. S. (2016). Building "our school": Parental perspectives for building trusting family-professional partnerships. *Preventing School Failure, 60,* 329–336.

Haines, S. J., Gross, J. M. S., Blue-Banning, M., Francis, G. L., & Turnbull, A. P. (2015). Fostering family-school and community-school partnerships in inclusive schools. *Research and Practice for Persons with Severe Disabilities, 40,* 227–239.

Harry, B. (2008). Collaboration with culturally and linguistically diverse families: Ideal versus reality. *Exceptional Children, 74,* 372–388.

Hewitt, A., Agosta, J., Heller, T., Cameron W. A., & Reinke, J. (2013). Families of individuals with intellectual and developmental disabilities: Policy, funding, services, and experiences. *Intellectual and Developmental Disabilities, 51,* 349–359.

Kyzar, K., Brady, Summers, J. A., & Turnbull, A. (2020). Family quality of life and partnership for families of students with deaf-blindness. *Remedial and Special Education, 41,* 50–62.

Kyzar, K. B., Turnbull, A. P., Summers, J. A., & Gomez, V. A. (2012). The relationship of family support to family outcomes: A synthesis of key findings from research on severe disability. *Research and Practice for Persons with Severe Disabilities, 37,* 31–44.

Mortier, K., Hunt, P., Desimpel, L., & Van Hove, G. (2009). With parents at the table: Creating supports for children with disabilities in general education classrooms. *European Journal of Special Needs Education, 24,* 337–354.

Peters, M. K., Felty, W. P., Kinney, S. K., Hudson, M. A., Fisher, M. J., & Wolraich, M. L. 9). Effective educational approaches to forging family-professional partnerships. *Inclusion, 7,* 244–253.

Reynolds, A. D., Crea, T. M., Medina, J., Degnan, E., & McRoy, R. (2015). A mixed methods case study of parent involvement in an urban high school serving minority students. *Urban Education, 50,* 750–775.

Positive Behavior Supports

Algozzine, B., Wang, C., & Violette, A. S. (2011). Reexaming the relationship between academic achievement and social behavior. *Journal of Positive Behavior Interventions, 13,* 3–16.

Bruhn, A. L., Kaldenberg, E., Tan, B. K., Brandsmeier, B., Rila, A., Lanphier, L., Lewis, M., & Slater, A. (2016). Examining the effects of functional assessment based interventions with high school students. *Preventing School Failure, 60,* 106–116.

Crone, D. A., Hawken, L. S., & Bergstrom, M. K. (2007). A demonstration of training, implementing, and using functional behavioral assessment in 10 elementary and middle school settings. *Journal of Positive Behavior Interventions, 9,* 15–29.

De Pry, R. L., & Sugai, G. (2002). The effect of active supervision and pre-correction on minor behavioral incidents in a sixth grade general education classroom. *Journal of Behavioral Education, 11,* 255–267.

Dietz, S. M., & Repp, A. C. (1973). Decreasing classroom misbehavior through the use of DRL schedules of reinforcement. *Journal of Applied Behavior Analysis, 6,* 457–463.

Feeney, T. J., & Achilich, J. (2014). Structured flexibility and context-sensitive behavioral support for the chronically cranky. *NeuroRehabilitation, 34,* 709–723.

Filter, K. J., & Horner, R. H. (2009). Function-based academic interventions for problem behavior. *Education and Treatment of Children, 32,* 1–19.

Greer, R. D., & Polirstok, S. R. (1982). Collateral gains and short term maintenance in reading and on-task responses by some inner-city adolescents as a function of their use of social reinforcement. *Journal of Applied Behavior Analysis, 15,* 123–139.

Hawken, L. S., O'Neill, R. E., & Macleod, K. S. (2011). An investigation of the impact of function of problem behavior on effectiveness of the Behavior Education Program (BEP). *Education and Treatment of Children, 34,* 551–574.

Inchley-Mort, S., Rantell, K., Wahlich, C., & Hassiotis, A. (2014). Complex Behaviour Service: Enhanced model for challenging behaviour. *Advances in Mental Health and Intellectual Disabilities, 8,* 219–227.

Ingram, K., Lewis-Palmer, T., & Sugai, G. (2005). Function-based intervention planning: Comparing the effectiveness of FBA indicated and contra-indicated interventions plans. *Journal of Positive Behavior Interventions, 7,* 224–36.

McCurdy, B. L., Lannie, A. L., & Barnabas, E. (2009). Reducing disruptive behavior in an urban school cafeteria: An extension of the Good Behavior Game. *Journal of School Psychology, 47,* 39–54.

Mitchell, R. R., Tingstrom, D. H., Dufrene, B. A., Ford, W. B., Sterling, H. E., & VanDer Heyden, A. (2015). The effects of the good behavior game with general-education high school students. *School Psychology Review, 44,* 191–207.

Myers, D. M., Simonsen, B., & Sugai, G. (2011). Increasing teachers' use of praise with a response-to-intervention approach. *Education and Treatment of Children, 34,* 35–59.

Nolan, J. D., & Filter, K. J. (2012). A function-based classroom behavior intervention using non-contingent reinforcement plus response cost. *Education and Treatment of Children, 35,* 419–430.

Oliver, R. M., Wehby, J. H., & Nelson, J. R. (2015). Helping teachers maintain classroom management practices using a self-monitoring checklist. *Teaching and Teacher Education, 51,* 113–120.

Sasso, G. M., Reimers, R. M., Cooper, L. J., Wacker, D., Berg, W., Steege, M., Kelly, L., & Allaire, A. (1992). Use of descriptive and experimental analyses to identify the functional properties of aberrant behavior in school settings. *Journal of Applied Behavior Analysis, 25,* 809–821.

Storey, K., Lawry, J. R., Ashworth, R., Danko, C. D., & Strain, P. S. (1994). Functional analysis and intervention for disruptive behaviors of a kindergarten student. *Journal of Educational Research, 87,* 361–370.

Turtura, J. E., Anderson, C. M., Boyd, R. J. (2014). Addressing task avoidance in middle school students: Academic behavior check-in/check-out. *Journal of Positive Behavior Interventions, 16,* 159–167.

Ylvisaker, M., Turkstra, L., Coehlo, C., Yorkston, K., Kennedy, M., Sohlberg, McKay. M., & Avery, J. (2007). Behavioural interventions for children and adults with behaviour disorders after TBI: A systematic review of the evidence. *Brain Injury, 21,* 769–805.

Social Supports

Brock, M. E., Biggs, E. E., Carter, E. W., Cattey, G., & Raley, K. (2016). Implementation and generalization of peer support arrangements for students with significant disabilities in inclusive classrooms. *The Journal of Special Education, 49,* 221–232.

Carter, E. W. (2017). The promise and practice of peer support arrangements for students with intellectual and developmental disabilities. *International Review of Research in Developmental Disabilities, 52,* 141–174.

Carter, E. W., Common, E. A., Sreckovic, M. A., Huber, H. B., Bottema-Beutel, K., Gustafson, J. R., Dykstra, J., & Hume, K. (2014). Promoting social competence and peer relationships for adolescents with ASD. *Remedial and Special Education, 35,* 27–37

Carter, E. W., Cushing, L. S., Clark, N. M., & Kennedy, C. H. (2005). Effects of peer support interventions on students' access to the general curriculum and social interactions. *Research and Practice for Persons with Severe Disabilities, 30,* 15–25.

Carter, E. W., Dykstra Steinbrenner, J. R., & Hall, L. J. (2019). Exploring feasibility and fit: Peer mediated interventions for high school students with autism spectrum disorder. *School Psychology Review, 48,* 157–169.

Carter, E. W., & Hughes, C. (2005). Increasing social interaction among adolescents with intellectual disabilities and their general education peers: Effective interventions. *Research and Practice for Persons with Severe Disabilities, 30,* 179–193.

Carter, E. W., & Pesko, M. J. (2008). Social validity of peer interaction intervention strategies in high school classrooms: Effectiveness, feasibility, and actual use. *Exceptionality, 16,* 156–173.

Carter, E. W., Sisco, L. G., Chung, Y., & Stanton-Chapman, T. (2010). Peer interactions of students with intellectual disabilities and/or autism: A map of the intervention literature. *Research and Practice for Persons with Severe Disabilities, 35,* 63–79.

Carter, E. W., Sisco, L. G., Melekoglu, M., & Kurkowski, C. (2007). Peer supports as an alternative to individually assigned paraprofessionals in inclusive high school classrooms. *Research and Practice for Persons with Severe Disabilities, 32,* 213–227

Hughes, C., Bernstein, R. T., Kaplan, L, M., Reilly, C. M., Brigham, N. L., Cosgriff, J. C., & Boykin, M. P. (2013). Increasing conversational interactions between verbal high school students with autism and their peers without disabilities. *Focus on Autism and Other Developmental Disabilities, 28,* 241–254.

Hughes, C., Carter, E. W., Hughes, T., Bradford, E., & Copeland, S. R. (2002). Effects of instructional versus non-instructional roles on the social interaction of high school students. *Education and Training in Mental Retardation and Developmental Disabilities, 37,* 146–162.

Hughes, C., Fowler, S. E., Copeland, S, R., Agran, M., Wehmeyer, M. L., & Church-Pupke, P. P. (2004). Supporting high school students to engage in recreational activities with peers. *Behavior Modification, 28,* 3–27.

Social Skills Instruction

Botsford, K. D. (2013). Social skills for youths with visual impairments: A meta-analysis. *Journal of Visual Impairment and Blindness, 107,* 497–508.

Francis, G. L., McMullen, V. B., Blue-Banning, M., & Haines, S. (2013). Increasing the social skills of a student with autism through a literacy-based behavioral intervention. *Intervention in School and Clinic, 49,* 77–83.

Gül, S. O. (2016). The combined use of video modeling and social stories in teachingsocial skills for individuals with intellectual disability. *Educational Sciences: Theory and Practice, 16,* 83–107.

Gül, S., & Vuran, S. (2010). An analysis of studies conducted video modeling in teaching social skills. *Educational Sciences: Theory and Practice, 10,* 249–274.

Hughes, C., Golas, M., Cosgriff, J., Brigham, N., Edwards, C., & Cashen, K. (2011). Effects of a social skills intervention among high school students with intellectualdisabilities and autism and their general education peers. *Research and Practice forPersons with Severe Disabilities, 36,* 46–61.

Hughes, C., Kaplan, L., Bernstein, R., Boykin, M., Reilly, C., Brigham, N., Cosgriff, J., Heilingoetter, J., & Harvey, M. (2012). Increasing social interaction skills of secondary school students with autism and/or intellectual disability: A review of interventions. *Research and Practice for Persons with Severe Disabilities, 37,* 288–307.

Lo, Y., Correa, V. I., & Anderson, A. L. (2015). Culturally responsive social skill instruction for Latino male students. *Journal of Positive Behavior Interventions, 17,* 15–27.

Lo, Y., Mustian, A. L., Brophy, A., & White, R. B. (2011). Peer-mediated social skill instruction for African American males with or at risk for mild disabilities. *Exceptionality, 19,* 191–209.

Marquez, B., Marquez, J., Vincent, C. G., Pennefather, J., Sprague, J. R., Smolkowski, K., & Yeaton, P. (2014). The iterative development and initial evaluation of We Have Skills!: An innovative approach to teaching social skills to elementary students. *Education and Treatment of Children, 37,* 137–161.

Self-Management Strategies

Hoff, K. E., & Ervin, R. A. (2013). Extending self-management strategies: The use ofa classwide approach. *Psychology in the Schools, 50,* 151–164.

Miller, B., & Taber-Doughty, T. (2014). Self-monitoring checklists for inquiryproblem-solving: Functional problem-solving methods for students with intellectual disability. *Education and Training in Autism and Developmental Disabilities, 49,* 555–567.

Moore, D. W., Prebble, S., Robertson, J., Waetford, R., & Anderson, A. (2001). Self-recording with goal setting: A self-management programme for the classroom. *Educational Psychology, 21,* 255–265.

Rock, M., & Thead, B. (2007). The effects of fading a strategic self-monitoring intervention on students' academic engagement, accuracy, and productivity. *Journal of Behavioral Education, 16,* 389–412.

Shogren, K. A., Lang, R., Machalicek, W., Rispoli, M. J., & O'Reilly, M. (2011). Self-versus teacher management of behavior for elementary school students with Asperger Syndrome: Impact on classroom behavior. *Journal of Positive Behavior Interventions, 13,* 87–96.

Sutherland, K. S., & Snyder, A. (2007). Effects of reciprocal peer tutoring and self-graphing on reading fluency and classroom behavior of middle school students with emotional or behavioral disorders. *Journal of Emotional and Behavioral Disorders, 15,* 103–118.

Trevino-Maack, S., Kamps, D., & Wills, H. (2015). A group contingency plus self-management intervention targeting at-risk secondary students' class-work and active engagement. *Remedial and Special Education, 36,* 347–360.

Wills, H., & Mason, B. (2014). Implementation of a self-monitoring application to improve on-task behavior: A high-school pilot study. *Journal of Behavioral Education, 23,* 421–434.

Self-Advocacy

Anderson, S., & Bigby, C. (2017). Self-advocacy as a means to positive identities for people with intellectual disability: 'We just help them, be them really'. *Journal of Applied Research in Intellectual Disabilities, 30,* 109–120.

Beckwith, R. M., Friedman, M. G., & Conroy, J. W. (2016). Beyond tokenism: People with complex needs in leadership roles: A review of the literature. *Inclusion, 4,* 137–155.

Burke, M. M., Goldman, S. E., Hart, M. S., & Hodapp, R. M. (2016). Evaluating the efficacy of a special education advocacy training program. *Journal of Policy and Practice in Intellectual Disabilities, 13,* 269–276.

Caldwell, J. (2010). Leadership development of individuals with developmental disabilities in the self-advocacy movement. *Journal of Intellectual Disability Research, 54,* 1004–1014.

Dryden, E., M., Desmarais, J., & Arsenault, L. (2014). Effectiveness of the impact: Ability program to improve safety and self-advocacy skills in high school students with disabilities. *Journal of School Health, 84,* 793–801.

Feldman, M. A.. Owen, F. Andrews, A. Hamelin, J. Barber, R. & Griffiths, D. (2012). Health self-advocacy training for persons with intellectual disabilities. *Journal of Intellectual Disability Research, 56,* 1110–1121.

Gilmartin, A., & Slevin, E. (2010). Being a member of a self-advocacy group: Experiences of intellectually disabled people. *British Journal of Learning Disabilities, 38,* 152–159.

Landmark, L. J., Zhang, D., Ju, S., McVey, T. C., & Ji, M. Y. (2017). Experiences of disability advocates and self-advocates in Texas. *Journal of Disability Policy Studies, 27,* 203–211.

Nonnemacher, S. L., & Bambara, L. M. (2011). "I'm supposed to be in charge": Self-advocates' perspectives on their self-determination support needs. *Intellectual and Developmental Disabilities, 49,* 327–340.

Roberts, E. L, Ju, S., & Zhang, D. (2016). Review of practices that promote self-advocacy for students with disabilities. *Journal of Disability Policy Studies, 26,* 209–220.

Self-Determination

Konrad, M., Fowler, C. H., Walker, A. R., Test, D. W., & Wood, W. M. (2007). Effects of self-determination interventions on the academic skills of students with learning disabilities. *Learning Disability Quarterly, 30,* 89–113.

Levin, D. S., & Rotheram-Fuller, E. (2011). Evaluating the empowered curriculum for adolescents with visual impairments. *Journal of Visual Impairment and Blindness, 105,* 350–360.

Martin, J. E., Mithaug, D. E., Cox, P., Peterson, L. Y., Van Dycke, J. L., & Cash, M. E. (2003). Increasing self-determination: Teaching students to plan, work, evaluate, and adjust. *Exceptional Children, 69,* 431–446.

Martin, J. E., Van Dycke, J. L., Christensen, W. R., Greene, B. A., Gardner, J. E., & Lovett, D. L. (2006). Increasing student participation in IEP meetings: Establishing the Self-Directed IEP as an evidenced-based practice. *Exceptional Children, 72,* 299–316.

Martin, J. E., Van Dycke, J. L., Greene, B. A., Gardner, J. E., Christensen, W. R., Woods, L. L., & Lovett, D. L. (2006). Direct observation of teacher-directed IEP meetings: Establishing the need for student IEP meeting instruction. *Exceptional Children, 72,* 187–200.

Seong, Y., Wehmeyer, M. L., Palmer, S. B., & Little, T. D. (2015). A multiple-group confirmatory factor analysis of self-determination between groups of adolescents with intellectual disability or learning disabilities. *Assessment for Effective Intervention, 40,* 166–175.

Shogren, K. A. (2011). Culture and self-determination: A review of the literature and directions for future research and practice. *Career Development for Exceptional Individuals, 34,* 115–127.

Shogren, K. A., Wehmeyer, M. L., & Palmer, S. B., & Paek, Y. (2013). Exploring personal and school environment characteristics that predict self-determination. *Exceptionality, 21,* 147–157.

Valenzuela, R. L., & Martin, J. E. (2005). The Self-Directed IEP: Bridging values of diverse cultures and secondary education. *Career Development for Exceptional Individuals, 28,* 4–14.

Wehmeyer, M. L., Palmer, S. B., Shogren, K., Williams-Diehm, K., & Soukup, J. H. (2013). Establishing a causal relationships between intervention to promote self-determination and enhanced student self-determination. *Journal of Special Education, 46,* 195–210.

Wehmeyer, M. L., Shogren, K. A., Zager, D., Smith, T. E., & Simpson, R. (2010). Research-based principles and practices for educating students with autism spectrum disorders: Self-determination and social interactions. *Education and Training in Autism and Developmental Disabilities, 45,* 475–486.

Woods, L. P., & Martin, J. E. (2013). The difference a year makes: An exploratory Self-Directed IEP case study. *Exceptionality, 21,* 176–189.

Person-Centered Planning

Claes, C., Van Hove, G., Vandevelde, S., van Loon, J., & Schalock, R. L. (2010). Person-centered planning: Analysis of research and effectiveness. *Intellectual and Developmental Disabilities, 48,* 432–453

Flannery, K. B., Newton, S., Horner, R. H., Slovic, R., Blumberg, R., & Ard, W. R. (2000). The impact of person centered planning on the content and organization of individual supports. *Career Development for Exceptional Individuals, 23,* 123–137.

Gosse, L., Griffiths, D., Owen, F., & Feldman, M. (2017). Impact of an individualized planning approach on personal outcomes and supports for persons with intellectual disabilities. *Journal of Policy and Practice in Intellectual Disabilities, 14,* 198–204.

LeRoy, B., Wolf-Branigin, M., Wolf-Branigin, K., Israel, N., & Kulik, N. (2007). Challenges to the systematic adoption of person-centered planning. *Best Practice in Mental Health, 3,* 16–25.

Miller, E., Stanhope, V., Restrepo-Toro, M., & Tondora, J. (2017). Person-centered planning in mental health: A transatlantic collaboration to tackle implementation barriers. *American Journal of Psychiatric Rehabilitation, 20,* 251–267.

Miner, C. A., & Bates, P. E. (1997). The effect of person centered planning activities on the IEP/transition planning process. *Education and Training in Mental Retardation and Developmental Disabilities, 32,* 105–112.

Ryan, B., & Carey, E. (2008). Introducing person-centered planning: A case study. *Learning Disability Practice, 11,* 12–19.

Inclusion Outside of the Classroom in the School

Carter, E. W. (2018). Supporting the social lives of secondary students with severe disabilities: Critical elements for effective intervention. *Journal of Emotional and Behavioral Disorders, 26,* 52–61.

Coster, W., Law, M., Bedell, G., Liljenquist, K., Kao, Y.-C., Khetani, M., & Teplicky, R. (2013). School participation, supports and barriers of students with and without disabilities. *Child: Care, Health and Development, 39,* 535–543.

Gaylord-Ross, R. J., Haring, T. G., Breen, C., & Pitts-Conway, V. (1984). The training and generalization of social interaction skills with autistic youth. *Journal of Applied Behavior Analysis, 17,* 229–247.

Kleinert, H. L., Miracle, S., & Sheppard-Jones K. (2007). Including students with moderate and severe disabilities in extracurricular and community recreation activities: Steps to success. *Teaching Exceptional Children, 39,* 33–38.

Kleinert, H. L., Miracle, S., & Sheppard-Jones K. (2007). Including students with moderate and severe intellectual disabilities in school extracurricular and community recreation activities. *Intellectual and Developmental Disabilities, 45,* 46–55.

Pence, A., & Dymond, S. (2015). Extracurricular school clubs: A time for fun and learning. *Teaching Exceptional Children, 47,* 281–288.

Pence, A. R., & Dymond, S. K. (2016). Teachers' beliefs about the participation of students with severe disabilities in schoolsponsored clubs. *Research and Practice for Persons with Severe Disabilities, 41,* 52–68.

Taylor, J., & Yun, J. (2012). Factor influencing staff inclusion of youth with disabilities in after-school programs. *Therapeutic Recreation Journal, 46,* 301–312.

Inclusion Outside of the School Setting

Carter, E. W., Harvey, M. N., Taylor, J. L., & Gotham, K. (2013). Connecting youth and young adults with autism spectrum disorders to community life. *Psychology in the Schools, 50,* 888–898.

Carter, E. W., Swedeen, B., Cooney, M., Walter, M. J., & Moss, C. K. (2012). "I don't have to do this by myself?": Parent-led community conversations to promote inclusion. *Research and Practice for Persons with Severe Disabilities, 37,* 9–23.

Carter, E. W., Swedeen, B., Moss, C. K., & Pesko, M. J. (2010). "What are you doing after school?" Promoting extracurricular involvement for transition-age youth with disabilities. *Intervention in School and Clinic, 45,* 275–283.

Dymond, S., Renzaglia, A., & Chun, E. (2008). Inclusive high school service learning programs: Methods for and barriers to including students with disabilities. *Education and Training in Developmental Disabilities, 43,* 20–36.

Dymond, S., Renzaglia, A., Chun, E., & Kim, R. (2013). A validation of elements, methods, and barriers to inclusive high school service learning programs. *Remedial and Special Education, 34,* 293–304.

Fennick, E., & Royle, J. (2003). Community inclusion for children and youth with developmental disabilities. *Focus on Autism and Other Developmental Disabilities, 18,* 20–27.

Koegel, R. L., Werner, G. A., Vismara, L. A., & Koegel, L. K. (2005). The effectiveness of contextually supported play date interactions between children with autism and typically developing peers. *Research and Practice for Persons with Severe Disabilities, 30,* 93–102,

Miller, K., Schleien, S., Kraft, H., Bodo-Lehman, D., Frisoli, A., & Strack, R. (2004). Teaming up for inclusive volunteering: A case study of a volunteer program for youth with and without disabilities. *Leisure, 28,* 115–136.

Schleien, S., Green, F., & Stone, C. (2003). Making friends within inclusive community recreation programs. *American Journal of Recreation Therapy, 2,* 7–16.

Schleien, S., & Miller, K. (2010). Diffusion of innovation: A roadmap for inclusive community recreation services. *Research and Practice for Persons with Severe Disabilities, 35,* 93–101.

Executive Functioning

Foy, J. G., & Mann, V. A. (2013). Executive function and early reading skills. *Reading and Writing: An Interdisciplinary Journal, 26,* 453–472.

Heyl, V., & Hintermair, M. (2015). Executive function and behavioral problems in students with visual impairments at mainstream and special schools. *Journal of Visual Impairment and Blindness, 109,* 251–263.

Jurado, M. B., & Rosselli, M. (2007). The elusive nature of executive functions: A review of our current understanding. *Neuropsychology Review, 17,* 213–233.

Ozonoff, S., & McEvoy, R. E. (1994). A longitudinal study of executive function and theory of mind development in autism. *Development and Psychopathology, 6,* 415–431.

Piovesana, A., Ross, S., Lloyd, O., Whittingham, K., Ziviani, J., Ware, R., McKinlay, L., & Boyd, R. (2017). A randomised controlled trial of a web-based multimodal therapy program to improve executive functioning in children and adolescents with acquired brain injury. *Clinical Rehabilitation, 31,* 1351–1363.

Royall, D. R., Lauterbach, E. C., Cummings, J. L., Reeve, A., Rummans, T. A., Kaufer, D. I., LaFrance, W. C., & Coffey, C. E. (2002). Executive control function: A review of its promise and challenges for clinical research. A report from the Committee on Research of the American Neuropsychiatric Association. *The Journal of Neuropsychiatry and Clinical Neurosciences, 14,* 377–405.

Spikman, J. M., Boelen, D. H., Lamberts, K. F., Brouwer, W. H., & Fasotti, L. (2010). Effects of a multifaceted treatment program for executive dysfunction after acquired brain injury on indications of executive functioning in daily life. *Journal of the International Neuropsychological Society, 16,* 118–129.

Stubberud, J., Langenbahn, D., Levine, B., Stanghelle, J., & Schanke, A. (2014). Goal Management Training improves everyday executive functioning for persons with spina bifida: Self-and informant reports six months post-training. *Neuropsychological Rehabilitation, 24,* 26–60.

Winsler, A., Abar, B., Feder, M., Schunn, C., & Rubio, D. (2007). Private speech andexecutive functioning among high-functioning children with autistic spectrum disorders. *Journal of Autism and Developmental Disorders, 37,* 1617–1635.

Use of Technology

Boyle, J. R., & Kennedy, M. J. (2019). Innovations in classroom technology for students with disabilities. *Intervention in School and Clinic, 55,* 67–70.

Chelkowski, L., Yan, Z., & Asaro-Saddler, K. (2019). The use of mobile devices with students with disabilities: A literature review. *Preventing School Failure, 63,* 277–295.

Clay, S. L., & Alston, R. (2016). The benefits of assistive technology use by persons with physical conditions: An examination of difficulty levels in areas of functioning. *Technology and Disability, 28,* 111–121.

Fage, C., Consel, C., Etchegoyhen, K., Amestoy, A., Bouvard, M., Mazon, C., & Sauzéon, H. (2019). An emotion regulation app for school inclusion of children with ASD: Design principles and evaluation. *Computers and Education, 131,* 1–21.

Ganz, J., Heath, A., Davis, J., & Vannest, K. (2013). Effects of a self-monitoring device on socially relevant behaviors in adolescents with Asperger disorder: A pilot study. *Assistive Technology: The Official Journal of RESNA, 25*(3), 149–157.

Ganz, J. B., Morin, K. L., Foster, M. J., Vannest, K. J., Genç T. D., Gregori, E. V., & Gerow, S. L. (2017). High-technology augmentative and alternative communication for individuals with intellectual and developmental disabilities and complex communication needs: S meta-analysis. *AAC: Augmentative and Alternative Communication, 33,* 224–238.

Lindsay, S., Kolne, K., Oh, A., & Cagliostro, E. (2019). Children with disabilities engaging in STEM: Exploring how a group-based robotics program influences stem activation. *Canadian Journal of Science, Mathematics and Technology Education, 19,* 387–397.

Satsangi, R., Miller, B., & Savage, M. N. (2019). Helping teachers make informed decisions when selecting assistive technology for secondary students with disabilities. *Preventing School Failure, 63,* 97–104.

Smith, S. J., Lowrey, K. A., Rowland, A. L., & Frey, B. (2020). Effective technology supported writing strategies for learners with disabilities. *Inclusion, 8,* 58–73.

Physical, Medical, Psychological, or Mental Health Issues

Ballard, S., & Dymond, S. (2016). Acquired severe disabilities and complex health care needs: Access to inclusive education. *Research and Practice for Persons with Severe Disabilities, 41,* 191–208.

Bernstein, A., Chorpita, B. F.; Rosenblatt, A., Becker, K. D., Daleiden, E. L., & Ebesutani, C. K. (2015). Fit of evidence-based treatment components to youths served by wraparound process: A relevance mapping analysis. *Journal of Clinical Child and Adolescent Psychology, 44,* 44–57.

Cosma, P., & Soni, A. (2019). A systematic literature review exploring the factors identified by children and young people with behavioural, emotional and social difficulties as influential on their experiences of education. *Emotional and Behavioural Difficulties, 24,* 421–435.

Dembo, R. S., & LaFleur, J. (2019). Community health contexts and school suspensions of students with disabilities. *Children and Youth Services Review, 102,* 120–127.

Mendenhall, A. N., Kapp, S. A., Rand, A., Robbins, M. L., & Stipp, K. (2013). Theory meets practice: The localization of wraparound services for youth with serious emotional disturbance. *Community Mental Health Journal, 49,* 793–804.

Murthy, M. S., Rajaram, P., Mudiyanuru, K. S., Palaniappan, M., Govindappa, L., & Dasgupta, M. (2020). Potential for increased epilepsy awareness: impact of health education program in schools for teachers and children. *Journal of Neurosciences in Rural Practice, 11,* 119–124.

Painter, K. (2012). Outcomes for youth with severe emotional disturbance: A repeated measures longitudinal study of a wraparound approach of service delivery in systems of care. *Child and Youth Care Forum, 41,* 407–425.

Shaw, L., Moore, D., Nunns, M., Thompson-Coon, J., Ford, T., Berry, V., Walker, E., Heyman, I., Dickens, C., Bennett, S., Shafran, R., & Garside, R. (2019). Experiences of interventions aiming to improve the mental health and well-being of children and young people with a long-term physical condition: A systematic review and meta-ethnography. *Child: Care, Health and Development, 45,* 832–849.

Collaboration

Blue-Banning, M., Summers, J. A., Frankland, H. C., Nelson, L., & Beegle, G. (2004). Dimensions of family and professional partnerships: Constructive guidelines for collaboration. *Exceptional Children, 70,* 167–184.

Carter, N., Prater, A., Jackson, A., Marchant, M. (2009). Educators' perceptions of collaborative planning processes for students with disabilities. *Preventing School Failure, 54,* 60–70.

Fenty, N. S., McDuffie-Landrum, K., & Fisher, G. (2012). Using collaboration, co-teaching, and question answer relationships to enhance content area literacy. *Teaching Exceptional Children, 44*(6), 28–37.

Huefner, D. S. (1988). The consulting teacher model: Risks and opportunities. *Exceptional Children, 54,* 403–414.

Lamar-Dukes, P., & Dukes, C. (2005). Consider the roles and responsibilities of the inclusion support teacher. *Intervention of School and Clinic, 41,* 55–61.

Noonan, P. M., Morningstar, M. E., & Erickson, A. G. (2008). Improving interagency collaboration: Effective strategies used by high-performing local districts and communities. *Career Development for Exceptional Individuals, 31,* 132–143.

Santoli, S., Sachs, J., Romey, E., & McClurg, S. (2008). A successful formula for middle school inclusion: Collaboration, time, and administrative support. *Research in Middle School Education, 32,* 1–13.

Sayeski, K. L. (2009). Defining special educators' tools: The building blocks of effective collaboration. *Intervention in School and Clinic, 45,* 38–44.

Solis, M., Vaughn, S., Swanson, E., & McCulley, L. (2012). Collaborative models of instruction: The empirical foundations of inclusion and co-teaching. *Psychology in the Schools, 49,* 498–510.

Legal Issues

Atkins, D. G., & Hayman, R. L. (2017). Disability and the law: An essay on inclusion, from theory to practice. *Widener Law Review, 23,* 167–185.

Blanck, P. (2019). Why America is better off because of the Americans with Disabilities Act and the Individuals with Disabilities Education Act. *Touro Law Review, 35,* 605–618.

Cemius, A. (2017). Enforcing the Americans with Disabilities Act for the "invisibly disabled": Not a handout, just a hand. *Georgetown Journal on Poverty Law and Policy, 25,* 35–73.

de Beco, G. (2018). The right to inclusive education: Why is there so much opposition to its implementation? *International Journal of Law in Context, 14,* 396–415.

Rakap, S., Yucesoy-Ozkan, S., & Kalkan, S. (2019). How complete are individualized education programmes developed for students with disabilities served in inclusive classroom settings? *European Journal of Special Needs Education, 34,* 663–677.

Silvers, A., & Francis, L. (2017). An Americans with Disabilities Act for everyone, and for the ages as well. *Cardozo Law Review, 39,* 669–698.

Turnbull, H. R., Turnbull, A. P., & Cooper, D. H. (2018). The Supreme Court, Endrew, and the appropriate education of students with disabilities. *Exceptional Children, 84,* 124–140.

Zirkel, P. A. (2020). An updated primer of special education law. *Teaching Exceptional Children, 52,* 261–265.

NAME INDEX

A

Abar, Beau, 64, 68, 144
Adams, Gary, 118
Able, Harriet, 135
Achilich, Jason, 137
Agosta, John, 136
Agran, Martin, 34, 38, 48, 50, 62, 66, 76,
        78, 89, 92, 116, 119, 139
Ahlgren, Charlotte, 117
Ahlgrim-Delzell, Lynn, 135
Albin, Richard, 31, 38, 59, 68, 85, 93, 134
Alborz, A., 121
Algozzine, Bob, 71, 78, 120, 137
Allaire, Ann, 138
Allport, Gordon, 15, 19
Alper, Sandra, 6, 19, 72, 80, 116
Alves, Kat, 77, 79
Alzrayer, Nouf, 64, 66
Amestoy, Anouck, 145
Anderson, Adrienne, 139
Anderson, Angelika, 140
Anderson, Cynthia, 138
Anderson, Philip, 24, 25
Anderson, Sian, 140
Andrews, A., 141
Appleton, Amanda, 72, 79
Ard, William, 142
Arsenault, Lisa, 141
Asaro-Saddler, Kristie, 145
Ashby, Christine, 116
Ashworth, Ruth, 138
Asmus, Jennifer, 67, 93, 117
Atkins, Daniel, 147
Attwood, Tony, 31, 38
Avery, Jack, 138
Ayala, Emiliano, 116

Ayres, Kevin, 53, 66
Azmitia, Margarita, 63, 66

B

Bagllieri, Susan, 5, 19
Bailey, Jenevie, 115
Baker, Diana, 133
Baker, Scott, 73, 80, 84, 93
Balcazar, Fabricio, 111
Ballard, Sarah, 117, 145
Bambara, Linda, 89, 93, 141
Banda, Devender, 64, 66
Barber, Ana, 72, 73, 78, 84, 93
Barber, R., 141
Barbetta, Patricia, 118
Barker, Heidi, 113
Barnabas, Ernesto, 137
Barrera, Manuel, 8, 19
Basham, James, 117
Bashinski, Susan, 121, 134
Bates, Paul, 62, 66, 134, 142
Bauby, Jean-Dominique, 111
Baumgart, Diane, 54, 66
Bay-Hinitz, April, 117
Becker, Kimberly, 145
Beckwith, Ruthie-Marie, 140
Bedell, G., 143
Beegle, Gwen, 146
Beers, Mary, 119
Bell, Christopher, 111
Bellamy, G. Thomas, 56, 66
Bender, Karen, 111
Bennett, Sophie, 146
Berg, Wendy, 138
Bergstrom, Melissa, 137
Berkeley, Sheri, 72, 73, 77, 78, 80, 84, 93

149

SUBJECT INDEX

ABOUT THE AUTHOR

Keith Storey, Ph.D., BCBA-D, is currently a Clinical Director at Juvo Autism and Behavioral Health Services in Oakland, California. He is also a Professor Emeritus at Touro University in Vallejo, California. Keith has over forty years' experience working with individuals with disabilities, including six years as a classroom teacher. His professional and research interests include transition from school to adult life, functional analysis and positive behavioral supports, supported employment, inclusion, and curriculum development. Keith is the recipient of the 1988 Alice H. Hayden Award from The Association for Persons with Severe Handicaps; the 1996 Hau-Cheng Wang Fellowship from Chapman University, which is presented for exceptional merit in scholarship; and the 2001 Robert Gaylord-Ross Memorial Scholar Award from the California Association for Persons with Severe Disabilities. He is a member of the Illinois State University College of Education Alumni Hall of Fame. He has published over 100 journal articles on a wide variety of topics. Keith has published the books *Positive Behavior Supports for Adults with Disabilities in Employment, Community, and Residential Settings: Practical Strategies that Work, Case Studies in Transition and Employment for Students and Adults with Disabilities, Positive Behavior Supports in Classrooms and Schools: Effective and Practical Strategies for Teachers and Other Service Providers, Case Studies in Applied Behavior Analysis for Students and Adults with Disabilities, Systematic Instruction of Functional Skills for Students and Adults with Disabilities, The Road Ahead: Transition to Adult Life for Persons with Disabilities, Walking Isn't Everything: An Account of the Life of Jean Denecke,* and *Functional Assessment and Program Development for Problem Behavior: A Practical Handbook.* He currently serves on the editorial boards of Journal of Vocational Rehabilitation, Education and Training in Autism and Developmental Disabilities, Journal of Positive of Behavior Interventions, and Research and Practice for Persons with Severe Disabilities. He previously served on the editorial boards of Career Development and Transition for Exceptional Individuals, Education and Treatment of Children, Vocational Evaluation and Career Assessment Professional Journal, and Exceptionality. Keith's amazon author page is at www.amazon.com/author/keithstorey and his Goodreads author page is at https://www.goodreads.com/author/show/105547.Keith_Storey. You can email him at keith.storey@tu.edu.